The Mass

An Invitation to Enjoy It

Amy Florian

ACTA

ASSISTING CHRISTIANS TO ACT

PUBLICATIONS

The Mass
An Invitation to Enjoy It
by Amy Florian

Edited by Kass Dotterweich and Gregory F. Augustine Pierce
Cover design by Tom A. Wright
Typesetting by Desktop Edit Shop, Inc.
Cover photo from the collection, Landscapes of the World, by Corel Professional Photos, used under rights granted to Seescapes Publishing.

Published by: ACTAPublications
Assisting Christians To Act
5559 W. Howard Street
Skokie, IL 60077
800-397-2282
www.actapublications.com

Library of Congress Card Number: 2003109365

ISBN: 0-87946-253-1

Printed in the United States of America

Year: 10 09 08 07 06

Printing: 10 9 8 7 6 5 4 3 2

Contents

Introduction

There is a story about a woman who frequently cooked a whole ham for her family's dinner. To prepare the ham before she put it in the oven, the woman made small slices in the ham into which she inserted cloves, and she poured a pineapple-and-brown-sugar mixture over the entire ham. She then cut off one end of it, threw the end away, and slipped the ham into the oven for the allotted baking time. One day the woman's daughter asked her why she always cut off one end of the ham. "I don't know," replied the woman. "My mother always did that, so I always do it too." The daughter, consumed with curiosity, phoned her grandmother and asked about the strange practice. Her grandmother, through peals of laughter, explained to her granddaughter that she always cut off the end because otherwise the ham was too big to fit into the pan she used!

There is a natural human desire to understand why we do what we do. This desire serves us well—preventing us, for instance, from mindlessly throwing away chunks of perfectly good ham. It also underlies the search that allows us to consciously choose, to fully participate, and to constantly grow. We are more alive, and therefore more human, when we refuse to simply go through the motions without understanding, without investment, and without commitment.

Why the Mass?

Most Catholics celebrate Mass weekly. For some, it is a daily practice. The Mass is the central ritual of the Catholic faith. But why? That is one of the most common questions asked about Catholicism by Catholics and non-Catholics alike.

The simplest answer to this question is that God invites us to the meal to fulfill what Jesus asked of us: to break the bread, share the cup and be nourished in body and soul so that we can carry on his mission in the world. However, while Jesus celebrated the Last Supper, he did not design or script the parts of

5

the ritual we know as "the Mass" today. Those things have evolved over the centuries and continue to evolve to the present day as we grapple with the best way to embody what Jesus intended.

If we truly understand the Mass, we understand everything that is important about being a disciple of Christ. We welcome the stranger, recognizing that we are all members of the same Body. We listen to the stories that illustrate and form our identity, our challenges, our hopes and our faith. We offer ourselves and our gifts to God, that all may be consecrated as the body and blood of Christ. We worship, giving praise and thanks to God for all that we have, and we ask God's protection, guidance and wisdom for ourselves and our world. We come to the table to become what we receive, fed and strengthened with the rest of the Body for the difficult task of the mission. Finally, we are sent out to do in the world what we have just practiced in the liturgy: to bring the peace and justice of God to the ends of the earth.

You're Invited to a Party

The way we celebrate the liturgy flows into and out of our daily lives. Imagine, for instance, a well-celebrated birthday party. The first thing we do is gather the community, the people who want to celebrate the presence of someone in our midst. We light candles signifying the number of years this person has brought light to our world. (As one gets older, of course, this can require quite a few candles!) We often pull out pictures from the past that illustrate the honored person's life and the impact he or she has had. We tell the stories, especially the favorites, and we remember what is truly important in life. We bring to memory those we love who are no longer physically present. We laugh, cry and hug, growing closer together as a result of our gathering.

No birthday celebration would be complete without singing. We who assemble do not sing "Happy Birthday" because we believe our voices are exceptional or because we are performing. Rather, we sing with joy and gusto to celebrate the

6

honored one in our midst.

And we bring gifts. We offer our time, our talent and our treasure, prompted by gratitude for what the person means to us and by a desire to give back some of the happiness we have received.

Finally, we all share in the one sweet bread that we call "cake."

By the time the party is over, everyone has been changed. Each person feels a deeper connection to the one whose life is being celebrated and to the entire community of family and friends. There is a subtle appreciation for our own lives and for the beloved people with whom we share them. There is often a sense of sadness for the passing of time, combined with a renewed determination to make today and tomorrow count. Most of the time, of course, we leave a birthday party not consciously aware of these changes. Yet they are real and they have significant impact on us.

We can easily discern these same dynamics in the rituals of Thanksgiving and Christmas, of family reunions and other everyday celebrations and meals. Like the Eucharistic Liturgy, each one contains elements of gathering, telling the stories, eating and drinking, and going forth with a new sense of identity and purpose.

Ever Changeless, Ever New

Like most birthday parties, the Mass follows a consistent structure each time we gather and celebrate it. Yet, although some of the words and most of the actions are the same each time, every liturgy is different. This difference is due partly to variations in the prayers we use, the scripture readings that are proclaimed, or the songs we sing.

Mostly, though, each Mass is different because every time we come to celebrate *we* are different. God continues to work in us through the liturgy and throughout the week. As we grow, we hear the words from varied perspectives with new understandings and new insights. Imagine, for instance, how dissimilar the experience of liturgy is for a seven-year-old First

Eucharist candidate, a teenager struggling to find identity and internal authority, a young married couple with their first child, a middle-aged man reflecting on his life, and an elderly woman facing terminal illness. Week after week, we are different people as we gather with the community. The circumstances and events of our lives affect our openness to the Spirit, our needs and desires, and our point of contact with God's grace.

This is as it should be, for the liturgy is not something separate from our lives. It is not the "holy time" at the beginning of our profane week. Rather, we bring our lives to the liturgy— our doubts, struggles, suffering and despair, as well as our beliefs, hopes, love and joys. We bring all that we are. There, in the fullness of liturgy, we join our life with the lives of the community and present them to God, who showers us with grace, forgives our sins, challenges us to transformation, and sends us back into the world to live as holy people.

The Promise of Transformation

Every time we celebrate Mass, we carry with us the memories and expectations that accompany our reunions, our birthday celebrations, our family dinners, and all the rituals of our daily lives. We bring the totality of our being to the celebration that connects us most deeply to the One who can make us whole. We come together at the table of the Lord, hoping to be renewed and transformed, healed and strengthened.

Of course, not every birthday or family ritual—and certainly not every Mass—is celebrated well. In fact, some gatherings are endured out of sheer duty. There are those people who refuse to fully participate or give themselves over to the action. And there are some who are so burdened by tension and resentments that, for them, true celebration is impossible. Some gatherings gradually become habitual, as people simply go through the motions. Yet every gathering carries the seed of hope that this celebration will be loving, renewing and transforming. That is, after all, the way it was intended to be, and something deep within us knows this.

When we celebrate Mass we are aware, too, that every

Catholic all over the world is participating in the same celebration. We are part of something much larger than ourselves, part of a Church universal. As we move through the liturgical years celebrating the same feasts again and again, we are aware that we are journeying toward the end of time, both in our physical lives and in the life of the world in which we live. We are part of the history of salvation, of the chosen people of God enacting the new creation in our daily lives. Although the ritual itself is ancient, the meaning is ever new.

And So We Begin

This book is for the inquirer coming to Catholicism for the first time, the non-Catholic spouse in a mixed-faith marriage, the lifelong Catholic whose last instruction on the Mass was many years ago, the college or high-school student seeking an appreciation of the liturgy, or the well-read adult Catholic seeking even more knowledge of this ritual that forms the core of Catholic faith life.

The following chapters explain the structure of the ritual, the pattern of feasts and seasons, and the connections and content of the readings we hear. We explore the ways in which Christ is present to us in our celebration and the implications that has for us as a gathered community. We look at when, why, and how we move, pray, and sing. Finally, we see that the end of the Mass is only the beginning, as we are sent out to live the liturgy in the world of our everyday lives.

In these pages, we explore the beauty, the power, and the infinite potential held within this most central ritual of the Catholic faith. The Mass can be lifeless and boring when it is not understood or celebrated well, and that is unfortunately a far too common experience. Yet the Mass can also be a compelling, transformative celebration, one that can literally change us and through us change the world. This is an invitation to enjoy that celebration.

Chapter One

The Framework and the Setting

Have you ever been to a play, a musical, an opera or any type of theater production? If so, you know there is a recognizable organization. There are large divisions called *acts*, with smaller divisions within each act called *scenes*. Knowing the act and the scene helps you see that particular part of the action within the context of the whole, which in turn helps you better understand the entire production.

Most people don't realize that the Mass is organized in the same way. There are four "acts": the Gathering Rite, the Liturgy of the Word, the Liturgy of the Eucharist, and the Dismissal. Within each of these acts there are several "scenes" that move the action along, inform and involve us, and lead us more deeply into prayer. If we understand these acts and scenes the entire experience of the Mass will make a lot more sense.

One caveat is in order. When we attend a theater production, we assemble as an *audience* whose role is to *watch* the production unfold before us. When we celebrate Mass, however, we are not the audience but the *actors*. Some of us have more visible parts or even spoken lines, but each person in the assembly is essential. We all have responses, actions and responsibilities in every one of the acts and scenes. We need to understand the flow and purpose of the ritual—not so we can follow the performance of others, but so we can participate fully, fulfilling our role in the celebration. We "go to" or "attend" a play. We *actively celebrate* Mass.

Act I: The Gathering Rite

When friends come over for dinner, we don't immediately sit down at the table and eat. Rather, we welcome our guests and make sure everyone is comfortable. There are often decorations indicating any special occasion being celebrated, and the guests mingle and talk. Once everyone is gathered and "in the mood," we begin the meal.

In a similar fashion, the Mass doesn't just plunge into the readings or the Eucharistic Prayer. Rather, we knit together as an assembly and prepare ourselves for what we are about to do. The Gathering Rite is a time of awakening, of becoming aware, of joining ourselves into a true assembly of worship.

Scene 1: The Procession and the Greeting

Like the raising of the curtain in the theater, the Procession is the official beginning of the liturgy, calling us to focus our attention. For Sunday liturgies, the Procession is usually accompanied by a gathering song. Unlike the passive listening that occurs when an overture at a musical production is played, the assembly at Mass participates in the gathering song, singing out as one voice to welcome the ministers and one another to the celebration.

After the presider shows reverence for the altar, he turns to the people and leads us in making the sign of the cross. This most holy and recognizable sign reminds us to whom we belong and recalls our baptism, when we were signed for Christ. (Many people also sign themselves with blessed water when they enter and leave the worship space, heightening the connection to baptism that is our entry point into worship and ministry.)

While it is tempting to swipe across your body absent-mindedly because the sign of the cross is such a familiar action, try slowing it down. Make a large, unhurried sign that sanctifies your whole body and marks you as a follower of Christ, committed to taking the cross upon yourself both as an individual and in solidarity with this faith community. It is a serious gesture; do it with thought and care.

After the sign of the cross, the presider offers a greeting, and the people respond. It isn't the usual "street greeting" ("How are you?" or "Good morning"), because this isn't an ordinary assembly. Usually, the words follow the examples of Saint Paul in his letters, wishing everyone peace and grace through Jesus Christ. Often the presider will then introduce the liturgy in words that act almost like a movie trailer, giving an overview of the readings we will hear, the feast we are celebrating, and the themes we can expect to hear in the next hour or so.

Scene 2: The Penitential Rite

Have you ever attended a play where the ending changes depending on what happens with the audience interaction? In the liturgy, the Penitential Rite can change every time. Eight versions are provided in the sacramentary, but the invocations can also be created by the presider to fit the day's celebration. The liturgy preparation team or the presider decides which options to use based on the feast, the readings, and the theme of the day.

Options include the following:

- The Confiteor is an ancient penitential prayer that begins with the words, "I confess to almighty God, and to you, my brothers and sisters, that I have sinned." The prayer recognizes our sinfulness both in what we have done and in what we have failed to do, and it asks the intercession of the community, both living and dead, on our behalf.
- The Penitential verses are two responsorial lines recognizing that we have sinned and asking for Christ's mercy and love.
- The Litany of Praise is a set of three invocations to Christ to which the assembly responds, using either the English responses, "Lord have mercy" and "Christ have mercy" or the original Greek "Kyrie eleison" and "Christe eleison." Contrary to popular belief, the invocations are not so much meant to ask forgiveness for our sins or faults as to recognize something Christ has done for us.

13

The idea is similar to a woman finding out she has won the lottery and exclaiming, "Lord, have mercy!" For instance, in one form of the prayer the presider says, "Lord Jesus, you came to call sinners," and we respond, "Lord, have mercy."

- A Sprinkling Rite is particularly appropriate during the Easter season. The presider and other ministers sprinkle the assembly with water from the font, reminding us of our baptism into Christ and our mission as disciples. If it's done properly, we should be prepared to get wet as we experience the symbol of death and new life.

The first three options end with the words of absolution spoken by the presider: "May almighty God have mercy on us, forgive us our sins, and bring us to everlasting life." The community gives its agreement by responding with a heartfelt "Amen."

At the conclusion of these options, we often recite or sing the *Gloria*, a festive hymn giving praise to God. The *Gloria*, however, is not used during Lent or Advent. In these times of waiting, renewing, and penitence, any proclamation of the *Gloria* would be like singing "Jeremiah was a bullfrog" at a graduation ceremony. The song simply doesn't fit the mood of the occasion.

Scene 3: The Opening Prayer

At a wedding reception, the best man offers a toast, gathering the wishes of all present into a succinct (preferably) "prayer" of hope and joy for the couple. Similarly, in the opening prayer of the liturgy, sometimes called a "Collect", the presider invites the assembly to pray. He then "collects" the spoken and unspoken prayers keenly felt in our hearts and offers them to our loving God. The assembly, rather than clinking glasses and saying "Here, here!" responds with "Amen," which means "I agree. So be it. Yes. Let it be so."

Act II: The Liturgy of the Word

The Liturgy of the Word is the storytelling part of the Mass. Most family gatherings involve stories. When we hear the legends of the family, the tales of our elders and the woes and mishaps of our relatives, we learn who we are as individuals and as a family. In the telling of our stories at Mass, we are formed as members of this particular family community, reinforcing what we believe, to whom we belong, and our relationship with others and with God. We sink our roots in the past and take on the challenges of the future. Hopefully, we also hear the currents of love that surge beneath every story told—love that binds us to one another through the ages.

Scene 1: The First Reading

All of the Scripture at Mass is proclaimed from an *ambo*, a raised podium with a flat or slanted top. *Ambo* comes from a Greek word that means "I ascend."

A lector (the Greek word *"lectio"* means "reader") proclaims the first reading. The text is usually from the Old Testament, the part of the Bible that existed before Jesus was born. (Scripture scholars are increasingly referring to these texts as the "Hebrew Scriptures." This term is much more respectful of our Jewish brothers and sisters, for whom these texts are not "old" but rather their living and "new" testament.) This reading regales, chastises and sometimes shocks us with stories of the chosen people as they awaited the coming of the Messiah.

The only time this reading is not from the Hebrew Scriptures is during the Easter season, when the first reading is from the Acts of the Apostles. The Book of Acts describes the emerging Church in the time after the resurrection and ascension, giving us important lessons and ideals of community life in light of our faith.

Listening to these stories is like listening to the history of our family. We hear about the heroes of our faith, those great figures who overcame incredible obstacles and sometimes sacrificed their lives to follow God. We learn where our ancestors in faith made mistakes so we can avoid them today. We learn how God has dealt with human beings in the past, and how our predecessors understood their relationship with God. We discover how Jesus fulfilled the predictions of a Messiah—for instance, as a suffering servant that brings salvation to a hungry world. We are reminded of God's faithfulness in spite of human frailty, of God's compassion and steadfast love.

This first reading always has a connection to the theme of the gospel. Pay attention to the reading, and see if you can determine the linking ideas. At the conclusion of the reading, the lector announces "The word of the Lord" and the assembly joyfully responds, "Thanks be to God."

Scene 2: The Responsorial Psalm

The next scripture proclamation is not a reading, but a song. It is from the Book of Psalms, the hymn book that formed the basis of Jewish worship in Jesus' day. These passages are intended to be sung in a responsorial fashion, where the cantor sings and the assembly responds. If these passages must be spoken, as often happens when there are no musicians present, the responsorial form usually is still used, forming a dialogue between the lector and the assembly. In some cases, the psalm may be read reflectively by the lector with music playing quietly in the background. At other times, it may be read antiphonally, with the two halves of the assembly reading alternating portions.

The Book of Psalms is filled with the longings, anguish, joys and hope of the authors. In these familiar verses, they poured out their hearts to God, trusting that God would always hear and answer them. The psalms vary in tone and emotion, ranging from "The Lord is my shepherd" to "My God, my God, why have you forsaken me?" As we sing, we join the psalmist in opening our hearts to God.

Scene 3: The Second Reading

The Second Reading, proclaimed by a lector, is from the New

Testament (increasingly called the "Christian Scriptures" for the same reason that the Old Testament is called the "Hebrew Scriptures"). Unlike the first reading, it only connects to the gospel theme during major feast seasons like Easter or Advent. Most of the time, it is a semi-continuous reading from the *"epistles"* or letters that Paul, Peter, James, or John wrote to various communities or individuals in the early Church. In other words, we take one letter, such as the one to the Ephesians, and read most of it in succession before going on to another.

Again there is an exception during the Easter season, when the Second Reading is either from the first letter of John or from the Book of Revelations. Revelations is a mystical book, full of symbolism and concerned with cosmic events and the end of the world. Throughout the Easter season, as we attempt to more fully understand the impact of the Resurrection, the stories of this book stimulate our collective imagination and speak to us about the universal power of God.

To help understand the purpose of the epistles, recall letters or e-mails you may have written to persons younger than yourself or to others you are mentoring. You probably answered their questions, offered advice, told them where you thought they were going wrong, or gave them support in what they were undertaking. The scriptural letters do the same thing, usually explaining doctrines or challenging errors, correcting community practices, and encouraging the listeners to faithfully live out their calling in Christ. The authors really cared about the people to whom they were writing, and they wrote with passion, conviction, and occasionally a bit of humor.

Letters like this never go out of date. Although some of the references to places or people no longer apply, the principles are universal and timeless. It's like finding a stirring letter your great-great-grandfather wrote to his fiancé about love and commitment. I know a couple who used just such a letter as part of their wedding ceremony; although the words were ancient they were truly words by which to live—no matter the time or the culture. In the same way, these scriptural readings can be as applicable to us today as they were two thousand years ago. We always need to be challenged, supported, corrected and loved.

Listen for the ways in which your attitude, faith or actions need to change to reflect your commitment to Christ.

At the end of the second reading, the lector concludes with, "The word of the Lord," and the assembly responds, "Thanks be to God."

Scene 4: The Gospel Acclamation

I remember sitting in the living room one day when my son burst into the room and shouted, "Listen, everybody! I've got big news!" Then he joyfully pranced around the room pretending to play a trumpet. Finally, he stood in the middle of the room and proclaimed, "Attention, attention! I have just been chosen to play the king in our school play!"

While my son's prelude was exaggerated in ways only a child can display, the truth is that we love to precede fabulous news by doing something flashy to attract everyone's attention. In the liturgy, the big news of the day is the Good News, the Gospel of our Lord Jesus Christ. We announce this momentous time by rising to our feet and singing a joyous "Alleluia!" (During penitential times such as Lent, the Alleluia is replaced with another acclamation of glory to God.)

The priest or the deacon and the assembly then wish the Lord's presence to one another. As the Gospel is announced, we make a triple cross on our forehead, lips and chest, asking that the words be understood with our minds, spoken on our lips, and believed in our hearts.

Scene 5: The Gospel

The climax of the storytelling has arrived. We listen eagerly to the clearest and most complete revelation of God in the person of Jesus Christ. The parables he tells, the miracles he performs and the teachings he offers are bread for our life. Some stories are very familiar—the prodigal son, the woman caught in adultery, the raising of Lazarus. Yet these are stories whose meaning can never be exhausted, with newness arising at every repetition.

Jesus' words are often difficult for us to accept. They may challenge our way of life, our attitudes and our goals. Many times we may get the same uncomfortable sinking feeling that chewed up our insides when a parent caught us doing something wrong. At other times, we can snuggle in as we would into our mother's lap, with Jesus offering a lighter burden and eternal peace. We need to listen carefully and let his words sink into our soul.

At the conclusion of the reading of the Gospel, the priest or deacon says, "The Gospel of the Lord," and in thanksgiving the assembly responds, "Praise to you, Lord Jesus Christ!" The Alleluia acclamation may be repeated in joyous seasons such as Easter and Christmas. The reader then kisses the book in a gesture of honor and respect, while silently asking that the words of the Gospel wipe away our sins.

Scene 6: The Homily

Do you remember the last time you saw a good movie? When a powerful film or show rolls around in your head, sparking your imagination and challenging you to think, don't you want to figure out what it means—as a work of art and as it applies personally to your own life? Aren't you anxious to talk about it with your spouse or friend or someone else afterwards?

The homily does the same thing for us. It is the preacher's tool to help the faithful "unpack" the lessons of the Mass and the Scripture. There is so much richness in the words we have just heard that it is impossible to take it all in. Yet if all we do is listen, without allowing our lives to be transformed by what we have heard, the words remain empty. In the homily, the preacher helps us focus on one or two aspects of the readings, interpreting them for us in light of biblical scholarship and helping us see how we need to change our attitudes and actions to more closely follow Christ.

Scene 7: The Profession of Faith

Now that we have heard and pondered the words of Scripture,

we stand as a united community to reaffirm our belief in the basic truths of our faith. We currently use the Nicene Creed, first created at the Council of Nicea in 325 in response to questions about Jesus' nature and identity. In liturgies where children are present, we sometimes use the Apostles' Creed. The entire assembly usually recites the Creed together, but it may also be professed in question-and-answer form, especially in liturgies when baptisms or confirmations are celebrated.

Why do we recite the Creed every Sunday? When our children were young, my husband and I developed a set of axioms that we would repeat to the kids until they knew them by heart. These axioms included things like: "I love you." "You can never do anything, no matter how awful, that will make me stop loving you." "I may be angry at you and hate what you did, but I will always, always love you."

Every time we said these things, our children heard the words and took them in, reinforcing their belief in our everlasting love for them. When they were tempted to doubt our love, our children could go back to those familiar words and reassure themselves, however tenuously, of the truth about our love. When we profess the Creed, especially when we do so with thought and active participation, we strengthen our faith and build the rock upon which we stand, a rock on which we can depend no matter what.

Scene 8: The General Intercessions or the Prayers of the Faithful

Since there are no pre-written official texts, these prayers are unique to each worshiping assembly, created by and for the members of the particular community. Ideally, the invocations are composed with the day's readings in one hand and the newspaper in the other, so they truly reflect the liturgy and the needs before us. In these prayers, we ask God's help for the Church, the world and its leaders, those oppressed or in need, and the local community. A lector or cantor proclaims the General Intercessions, and the assembly responds in word or song, often with a refrain similar to "Lord, hear our prayer."

Act III: The Liturgy of the Eucharist

The Liturgy of the Eucharist is what we have been preparing for all along. It is the peak and most important time of our celebration—the consecratory thanksgiving and meal. It mirrors all our usual mealtime activities: setting the table, saying grace, dividing up the portions, eating and drinking, and closing with prayer.

Scene 1: The Preparation of the Gifts

When my children were growing up, they rotated through the assigned task of "table-setter," taking responsibility to prepare the table so we could eat together. In preparation for sharing our community meal, we do the same. Members of the assembly cover the table with a cloth, if that has not already been done, and they bring the gifts of bread and wine that we offer to God. Of course, you know that when you give a gift to another person, you give a piece of yourself. In the same way, we symbolically place ourselves on the altar along with the gifts, so that as the bread and wine is transformed into the body and blood of Christ, we are transformed as well.

After receiving the gifts and offering prayers that bless God's goodness, the presider often washes his hands. This practice carries over from the early Church when people brought gifts ranging from food to animals, making it not only practical but also necessary for the presider to wash after receiving them. This cleansing is no longer necessary, but the gesture still reflects the desire for this celebration to wash away our sins and renew us in Christ.

Finally, the priest offers the prayer over the gifts, signifying that they and we are prepared to enter into the Eucharistic Prayer, during which the bread and wine will be transformed into the body and blood of our Lord.

Scene 2: The Greeting and the Preface

As you might guess by its name, the Preface is the introduction to the Eucharistic Prayer. It is similar to the introduction of a speaker at a banquet in which the speaker is praised and thanked and everyone is readied for the speech that will follow. To prepare us to pray as one, the presider uses one of seventy-four different Prefaces to speak of God's greatness and power and of our desire to join together in praise. As he ends, the presider invites the entire assembly to join with the saints and angels to sing of God's wonder and to bless the One who comes in the name of the Lord. With one voice, we sing or recite the "Holy, Holy."

Scene 3: The Eucharistic Prayer

The Greek word *eucharistia* means "thanksgiving." Within this great prayer, we thank and praise God for all of creation and for our salvation. The presider speaks Jesus' words from the Last Supper, and the entire assembly responds by proclaiming the mystery of faith, affirming our belief in the life, death and res-urrection of Jesus. The presider asks the Holy Spirit to bless and sanctify both the gifts and the people gathered. He prays for the Church and for the entire community, both living and dead. As we pray, we consecrate the bread and wine, transforming them from our simple gifts of bread and wine into the body and blood of Christ.

Because this is such an important prayer, there are many options: four standard Eucharistic Prayers, plus two for recon-ciliation, three that may be used in the presence of children, and four more for special needs, as well as variations for funer-al liturgies and other special occasions. Each of these options has a special emphasis, allowing the presider to choose based on the needs and circumstances surrounding that particular cel-ebration of the Mass. In other words, this selection allows him the kind of flexibility you have when you carefully choose just the right greeting card, poem or book to give to someone you love.

I recently attended the graduation at my son's college. The ceremony included a speech that touched the hearts and gave voice to the needs, desires and hopes of the people gathered.

When the address ended, everyone applauded and shouted, signifying their agreement and unity with what had just been spoken. In this same way, we end the Eucharistic Prayer on a celebratory and unifying note. The presider lifts the body and blood of Christ for all to see and loudly proclaims that all glory and honor belongs to God forever, through Christ and the Holy Spirit. The assembly, in agreement and unity with all that has just been spoken, responds as one voice with a great and joyous "Amen!"

Scene 4: The Communion Rite

The Lord's Prayer is one of the most recognized prayers in all of Christianity. As we recite or sing this prayer in the liturgy, it forms a wonderful transition between the Eucharistic Prayer and the meal, summarizing what we have just prayed and leading us on to the sign of peace, the communion meal, and our mission.

In the introduction to the Sign of Peace, the presider reminds us that Christ left a legacy of peace that transcends human divisions and difficulties and binds us together. In light of the biblical instruction to reconcile with our sisters and brothers before coming to the Eucharistic table (and perhaps knowing what it's like to sit down for a meal next to someone with whom we have a disagreement), we are invited to offer a sign of that peace to each other, extending our hands and our hearts to those we know—and to those we do not know.

The Sign of Peace is followed by what is called the Fraction Rite. If you have studied math, you know that a *fraction* is a part of the whole. As we recite or sing the Lamb of God (*Agnus Dei* in Latin), the one loaf is broken into many pieces and the one flagon of consecrated wine is distributed into many cups.

Our last act before going forward to the table is to offer a prayer based on the words the centurion spoke when he asked Jesus to heal his servant: "Lord, I am not worthy to receive you, but only say the word and I shall be healed" (see Matthew 8:8). Although we are in constant need of God's nourishment and healing, there is nothing we can do to earn the right to receive the gift God so generously sets before us. In humility and gratitude, therefore, we process forward as a community to share the one Bread of Life and the one Cup of Salvation, so that we may be transformed into the very body and blood we eat and drink. We walk in faith, receiving that which looks to be mere bread and wine but which we believe is the one true and living God, delivered up on a cross that we may live.

The Communion Rite ends when the presider offers a prayer that this meal may nourish the entire assembly in mind and heart and strengthen us for the task ahead.

Act IV: The Dismissal Rite

We have gathered as a community. We have remembered and received the challenge inherent in our story as the People of God. We have offered to God our gifts—the bread, the wine, and our very selves—that have become the body and blood of Christ. We have prayed our petitions, our thanks and our praise, and we have shared in the meal. It is now time to go. We may wish it didn't have to be over just yet. But we are not called to remain where we are. We are called to go out and live the Mass in our world.

Scene 1: The Greeting and the Blessing

One final time, the presider and the assembly wish the presence of the Lord for each other. The presider then blesses the assembly in the name of the Father, the Son and the Spirit.

Scene 2: The Words of Dismissal

When we leave family celebrations or gatherings, no one routinely challenges us to go out and change our lives. The Mass, however, is different. The point is not simply the experience itself but the difference it makes in our lives during the week. If celebrating the liturgy doesn't help us become better Christians, then it is an empty rite.

So at the close of the liturgy, the presider offers those most important and challenging words: "Go in peace to love and serve the Lord." The assembly responds, "Thanks be to God," not—we hope—in gratitude for the end of a tedious celebration but in thanksgiving for the strength gained from the Mass that empowers us to go out and live as disciples in the world.

The Mass has the power to change us profoundly. When we leave Mass, we are sent forth as transformed people charged with the responsibility to witness to and live out the faith we have just professed. We are commissioned to continue being the face, hands, arms and feet of Christ to a broken and hurting world.

Scene 3: The Procession

Filled, renewed and re-energized, the assembly files out to help bring the reign of God into being "on earth as it is in heaven." For most of us, the first challenge to our resolve will occur before we even exit the parking lot!

Questions for Reflection and Discussion

1. Describe a recent time when you gathered for a dinner party or family reunion. What happened as people arrived? What elements of story and meal were involved in the event? How did the gathering end?

2. Many parishes provide missalettes from which some people read during the Scripture Proclamation. The recommended practice, however, is to look at the lector and actively listen rather than reading along from the printed words. Can you articulate the difference between the two ways of receiving the Scripture and the reasons behind the recommendation to listen rather than read along?

3. Describe an effective gathering rite you have experienced at a liturgy. How did it help the assembly come together and prepare for the rest of the Mass?

4. During what part of the Mass are you the most engaged? When do you most struggle to stay attentive? Why do you think this is?

5. What invocations did your assembly lift up to God at the Mass you most recently celebrated? If you were to write a set of invocations for the liturgy next weekend, what would they be?

Chapter Two

Marking Time

As I was growing up, I was keenly aware of the passing of time. Every year my mother would buy a seemingly immense calendar, making sure the design provided plenty of room for her to write the daily schedule of engagements, responsibilities, parties, birthdays and other activities for my nine siblings and me. I learned the progression of time by watching Mom cross off days as they passed or count the days until some special event, and I appreciated the tidy rows of days and weeks. It was always an event when we turned the entire page to find a new month. The new page brought a unique and beautiful picture that often elicited "oohs" and "aahs" from the younger children. It also brought a fresh collection of carefully marked appointments and commitments, a microcosm of the events that held priority in our family and thus shaped our identity and purpose.

The cycle of seasons was another form of marking the passage of time in my childhood. I grew up in a rural and heavily agricultural community, and the pulse of the community flowed with the seasons. Spring was a frantic, exciting time, as the ground was freshly turned, prepared and planted. With the heat of summer came hay baling, cultivating crops, and prayers for rain as projections of the harvest were made, revised, and then revised again. Fall brought a whirlwind of activity—harvesting, making silage, and preparing both people and animals for what lay ahead. Winter was a time of cocooning, assessing the past year and planning for the next. Then the cycle started all over again.

Because of these youthful experiences, marking time in the liturgical year has a familiar, comfortable feel to it. I still get excited every year as we pass through the seasons, feasts and celebrations, telling and re-telling the ancient yet ever-new stories of our faith as we allow the God who is beyond all time to work in our hearts.

A Time to Get Ready

In Western culture, January 1 is New Year's Day, the first day of a calendar year. The "New Year's Day" of the Catholic Church, however, does not parallel that of our conventional calendar. Rather, the first day of the new liturgical year is the First Sunday of Advent, which falls on the Sunday closest to November 30. The Latin word *adventus* means "an approach" or "a drawing near." During the season of Advent, as we draw near to the celebration of Christmas, we allow God to "prepare the way of the Lord," to "make straight the paths" of our hearts so they may ever more fully welcome Christ. The bluish-purple and rose colors of Advent are warm and womb-like, inviting us into the lush mystery of birth and incarnation.

We start off each new liturgical year by looking back at the year just past. Thus, the readings on the First Sunday of Advent concern the end of the world, the same theme that was covered in the last several Sundays of the previous year. For some people, these readings serve as a warning, a reminder that judgment day will come. But the readings are also hopeful, affirming that we are part of a picture much larger than ourselves. We are part of salvation history—all of our stories join with those of the past and those yet to come as we march forward toward eternity.

The Second Sunday of Advent introduces John the Baptist, the messenger of Jesus who calls us to repent and prepare for the Messiah. Sometimes I think of him the way I remember my teacher prepping our class before a visit from the district superintendent. We knew someone very important was coming, as she scurried around preparing the entire room, making sure every child's hair was combed and issuing reminders of proper behavior and speech. John the Baptist, of course, was a great deal more forgiving about outward appearances, since he was the kind of guy who dressed himself in camel hair and ate grasshoppers. Yet he tells us of a visitor much more important than any school administrator, and he calls us to a much more substantial and long-lasting change than a clean room and combed hair.

The readings on the Third Sunday of Advent continue the story of John the Baptist, but with intensified hope and joy at the approach of the Light of the World. In fact, we call it *Gaudete Sunday,* which means "Sunday of Joy" or "Sunday of Rejoicing," and we light a rose-colored candle in the Advent wreath to indicate our anticipation. The readings also erase any doubt about the relative importance of John and Jesus. John is the messenger, while Jesus is the awaited Chosen One, whose sandal straps John is unworthy even to untie.

The Fourth Sunday of Advent tells the familiar events just prior to Jesus' birth. The excitement builds as the angel appears to Mary or the baby in Elizabeth's womb jumps for joy or Joseph receives divine instruction in a dream. Like a child in the back seat of a car who breathlessly asks, "Are we there yet?" we prepare for the imminent celebration of the transcendent God being born into our midst.

A Child Is Born

Our season of "drawing near" reaches its fulfillment when we surround ourselves with the white and gold colors of Christmas and retell the incredible story of Jesus' birth. We marvel with the shepherds, sing with the angels and fall down in awe before God. Most of all, we ponder anew the wondrous miracle that God chose to become human. We explore the truth that by taking on our flesh, God raises the dignity of all humanity and indeed all creation, making it possible for us to share in God's divinity. The Incarnation of Jesus Christ is our gift, our privilege and our responsibility.

Throughout the Christmas season, we immerse ourselves in these mysteries. On January 1 we celebrate the Feast of Mary the Mother of God, honoring the woman whose assent made Jesus' birth humanly possible. On the weekend following Christmas we keep the Feast of the Holy Family. We remember that our families are holy as well and that we are all called to bring Jesus into the world.

The next week we journey with the wise men as they faithfully follow the star. I remember when I traveled a distance to see Halley's Comet in 1986, but I'm not sure I would have the courage to follow a star so far away from my home and across many countries without even knowing where it was leading. Yet the wise men did, resulting in the *Epiphany*, which means "manifestation" or "showing." They found the Son of God manifested as an infant, lying in a manger (a food trough for animals) as if ready to feed a hungry world.

On the final feast of the Christmas season, the Baptism of the Lord, we open our ears and hearts to the Beloved Son. As the water of baptism is poured over him, we commit ourselves to listening to and following him, even though we know he is beginning the mission that will lead him to Calvary.

Isn't That Special?

After the Christmas season, there is a short period of Ordinary Time. Most people think this means that there are no feasts. Actually, there are several feasts celebrated during Ordinary Time, but because they are not major feasts the season itself can be called "ordinary." The origin of the term *Ordinary Time*, however, comes from the Latin word *ordinal*, which means "numbered." We therefore designate the Sundays in Ordinary Time by their numbers, beginning with the Sundays following the Christmas season, interrupted by Lent and Easter, and resuming again until we reach the very end of the liturgical year with the Thirty-Fourth Sunday in Ordinary Time.

Because Ordinary Time is not a high feast season, it can be more reflective and peaceful. During this time, we surround ourselves with green colors, so that just as trees "leaf out" and plants stretch their stalks toward the sun, we may grow more deeply in our understanding of faith and discipleship.

Ashes to Ashes, Dust to Dust

What stands out in your childhood memories of Lent? I recall most vividly the somber tone of the season, emphasized by purple color everywhere and the traditional "giving up" of something (usually candy or desserts). Although I didn't fully understand the value of denying myself something (except as a challenge with my sister, Kate, to see who could last the longest without sneaking a little bite of chocolate), even as a child I knew Lent was a time of repentance and change. The ashes distributed on Ash Wednesday symbolized most graphically that our bodies are temporary vessels made out of "dust" that will return to "dust."

The colors and activities of Lent leave no doubt that it is a penitential season of self-examination, sacrifice and transformation. The entire assembly is encouraged to practice spiritual disciplines: to fast, pray and give alms. Most parishes offer reconciliation services, missions, evening prayer, additional daily Masses and other opportunities for growth and prayer.

Too often we look at these spiritual disciplines as nothing more than rules we have to follow if we are to be "good Catholics." However, such an approach misses the point entirely. Our Lenten fasting is not a requirement of "membership in the club." Nor is our fasting aimed primarily at giving up candy or prejudice or negative habits in an effort to make ourselves into better, more acceptable people. Our fast should be first and foremost a "fasting of the heart," a way in which we allow God to work within us at our deepest, most vulnerable level.

It is not our job to save ourselves. That initiative comes from God. Our job is to cooperate with God's grace, healing and love. Lent does not mean we work especially hard to be good people; it means we invite God to work especially hard within us, to remove our "hearts of stone" and replace them with "hearts of flesh," to put sinew and muscle onto our "dry bones," and to bring us from death to life. Lent is a time to return to the Lord with our whole hearts, to open ourselves to the great work God has already begun in us, and to accept the love God longs to pour out upon us.

Hearing the Story

The first two Sundays of Lent always have the same gospel stories. On the first Sunday of Lent is the temptation of Jesus in the desert, when Jesus resists the devil's ploys to place the concerns

31

of this world above God. On the second Sunday of Lent, Jesus is transfigured as God's voice challenges us to listen to this "Beloved Son," who will reach his glory only by bearing the cross.

The readings for the next three Sundays of Lent vary, depending on the lectionary cycle (see the chapter "Telling a Great Story" for a discussion of the lectionary cycle). The final Sunday of Lent is called *Palm Sunday* or *Passion Sunday*. The liturgy opens with a triumphant palm-waving march into Jerusalem, continues with a reading of the Passion narrative and concludes with the Eucharistic meal.

Reliving the Promise

Perhaps you are married and have had the experience of attending a wedding. As you celebrate with the blushing bride and groom, you can't help but recall your own wedding. As the husband and wife pronounce their vows, you hear in your heart the echo of your own marriage vows and reflect on how different your journey of marriage has been from what you imagined it would be. You find yourself offering fervent prayers for this couple, hoping they might avoid some of your mistakes and find true and lasting happiness with each other.

During Lent, we have the opportunity for a similar but even more intense experience with the catechumens—those people seeking baptism and initiation into the Catholic Church. Having already been through months of teaching and discernment, the catechumens who are ready to become fully initiated now celebrate the Rite of Election. From that time on, they are called "the elect." During the Sundays of Lent the elect go through concentrated preparation, celebrating several rites with the community. For instance, on the Third, Fourth and Fifth Sundays of Lent, the elect engage in "scrutinies," kneeling in the midst of the community and asking to be delivered from whatever blocks their path to Christ.

The Lenten rites for the elect are structured for the benefit of the entire community and compel us to join in them wholeheartedly. Just as married couples relive their vows when they attend a wedding, in the rites of the elect all Christians can relive their decision to be active members of the Church. As we do so, we reflect on our own journey of faith—on the turbulent times when we find it hard to believe that God even exists and on the joyous times when we feel enfolded in God's embrace and blessed beyond measure. After these initiates are baptized, confirmed, and receive the Eucharist at the Easter Vigil, we find ourselves offering fervent prayers that we may all together find true and lasting happiness as members of the Catholic community of faith.

Short, but Oh, So Sweet!

Triduum is the shortest season of the liturgical year. *Tri* means "three," and *duum* means "days." Therefore, *Triduum* means "three days." They are Holy Thursday, Good Friday, and Holy Saturday/Easter Sunday. (Now, if you're counting by Western reckoning, you may insist that Thursday through Sunday is four days, not three. The difference is that the Hebrews counted days from sunset to sunset. Therefore, Thursday evening until Friday evening is one day, Friday evening until Saturday evening is two days, and Saturday evening until Sunday evening is three days.)

Despite its brevity, Triduum is the most important season, the "high holy days" of Christianity. It is during Triduum that we remember and celebrate the central core of our faith: the life, death and resurrection of Jesus (also called the Paschal Mystery). If it were not for the events of these days, there would be no Christianity. Jesus would be remembered as a very good and holy man, but not as our Savior and Lord.

Triduum is actually intended to be one continuous celebration. Each liturgy ends without a dismissal; the assembly is simply asked to stay in private prayer and reflection until gathering again the next day.

I'm Supposed to Wash What?

This short season wastes no time getting to the heart of the matter, as the very first celebration challenges all of our ideas of power and leadership. On Holy Thursday (also called Maundy Thursday in some traditions), Jesus, the Messiah and Lord, stoops down and washes the feet of his followers. Imagine the CEO of a huge company like Exxon or IBM washing the feet of each person at a meeting of the board of directors. It flies in the face of everything we are taught. American society tells us that power means domination, control and one-upmanship—being served (and feared) by everyone deemed below your position.

Jesus tells us that we've got it all wrong, that true power requires serving others. We are never to get so full of ourselves or so proud that we won't bend over and wash the dirty feet of a fellow human being. We are to lead by attending to the needs of others rather than by climbing over them on our way up the rungs of the ladder of success and prestige. We are never to abuse or misuse our authority, for we are called to servant leadership, not cut-throat power.

Death Comes to Call

On Good Friday we squarely face the consequences of following Jesus: We're heading to the cross. We hear the story from Isaiah about the suffering servant who is offered up for the sins of many. We sing a psalm of surrender in the midst of trials. We listen to the Passion narrative from the Gospel of John, walking with Jesus from his last meal with the disciples, to the Garden of Gethsemane, through interrogations and torture, and finally up the hill of Calvary, where he pours out his life for those he loves.

On the one hand, we are convicted of our own sin, of the times we have crucified the people who challenge us or dismissed those whose message was too hard to hear. On the other hand, we are asked to accept the cross that comes with discipleship, the certainty that we will face suffering, trials and even death. If we dare to embrace it, we walk forward with trembling hearts to venerate the cross.

God Always Gets the Last Word

Easter Vigil is the joyous proclamation of the Resurrection. We emerge from the darkness of the tomb and welcome the Light of the World, the light that dispels the shadows and brings new life where only death reigned. In an extended series of Scripture readings, we hear the story of salvation, from creation onward, reliving again the promises of God. We celebrate the initiation of the elect who have prepared to enter fully into the Catholic community, rejoicing at their baptism, confirmation and first Eucharist. Finally, we come to the table ourselves to fill our ancient hungers with the living bread and the cup of life.

Alleluia!

Christ is risen! Because we cannot possibly comprehend the depth and implications of our joyful proclamation in only one day, Easter is a fifty-day season that extends from the Easter Vigil until Pentecost (the word *pentecoste* in Latin means "fifty"). This season serves somewhat like a honeymoon does for a newly married couple. It is a special time set aside so that the events just celebrated have a chance to sink in and become daily reality.

Throughout this uplifting and joyous season, we continue to celebrate and explore the Paschal Mystery. It is a time of *Mystagogy*, which literally means "the art of interpreting mysteries." We hear stories about the birth of the new Church and the call to discipleship. We remember our own initiation into the Church, accompanied by the symbols of water, oil and flame. We deepen our understanding of faith, our commitment to live in community as the Body of Christ, and our resolve to bear the cross in order to follow Christ. To close the season, we celebrate the outpouring of the Spirit on the followers of Jesus, celebrated on the Feast of Pentecost, and pray that we too may have the strength and wisdom to bear the Good News to the world.

The Lazy Days of Summer?

The celebration of Ordinary Time following the Easter season begins with two major feasts: the Feast of the Holy Trinity and the Feast of the Body and Blood of Christ. This season ends in late November with the major feast of Christ the King. In between, all through the spring, summer and fall, there is extended Ordinary Time for reflection on the life and teachings of our Lord.

The lengthy period of Ordinary Time reminds me of the biographical shows on television—A & E's *Biography* and similar offerings. The shows often focus on people who lived in relative obscurity until they made a major scientific discovery or committed a horrific crime or somehow broke onto the worldwide scene. The purpose of any given biography is to examine a person's past, upbringing, relationships and writings in an attempt to figure out who that person was and what led that person to his or her newsworthy climax.

So far in the liturgical year, we have heard the "big" stories of Jesus' birth, death and resurrection. Ordinary Time is when we find out what happened in between, when we discover who Jesus was and what he taught. It is also a time of challenge, as we hear the parables, commands and teachings that confront us with the true meaning of discipleship. Those who have the courage to listen and take this season seriously will surely change their lives as a result.

Questions for Reflection and Discussion

1. What are the important "marker" events in your life? What do you do to remember those events?

2. There are times when the seasons of the Church conflict with the seasons of our culture. For instance, while we are still in Advent, the rest of the world is already celebrating

"the holiday season." By the time we reach Christmas and are ready to celebrate, others are putting their Christmas decorations away. What can we as Catholics do to be true to the story of faith while not acting like Scrooge toward the rest of the world?

3. What is your favorite liturgical season? Why?

4. Do you use colors, symbols, calendars or other devices to bring an awareness of the liturgical seasons into your home? If not, can you think of at least one thing you can do?

5. When you imagine Jesus, how do you see him? Do you picture Jesus as a baby or young child, as a teacher and healer with his disciples, as a suffering man being paraded through the streets and then hanging on a cross, or as a resurrected Christ? How do the various liturgical seasons affect the primary images you have?

Chapter Three

Telling a Great Story

I once attended a fabulous keynote speech at a conference. The speaker talked for over an hour about the challenges facing the Church today and the virtues we must cultivate to meet them. As soon as the speaker was finished, the audience jumped to their feet and gave her a long and rousing ovation.

Afterwards, I asked five people to summarize the talk and outline its main points. Not surprisingly, I got five very different responses. Although we all heard the exact same speech, we each heard the talk from our own perspective. We each listened for the topics that most concerned our particular parish or community. We each heard the words through the lens of our own personal experience and interpreted the speaker's remarks in light of our own biases, hopes and fears.

I know too that if each of us delivered our outlines to various groups and organizations in the weeks after the conference, we would vary our presentations depending on the audience, emphasizing the things that most concerned the group to which we were speaking. For instance, if one of us talked to a group of parents, he would focus on issues connected to the family and raising children. If another spoke to a parish staff, she would focus on community building, worship and faith formation.

Tell Me What Happened

The same dynamic occurs with the Gospels. There are four Evangelists, or gospel writers: Matthew, Mark, Luke and John. For several decades before the Gospels were compiled, the stories and quotes of Jesus were passed down through oral tradition or compiled in short stories passed around among Christian communities. When each writer, inspired by the Spirit, sat down to compose a "gospel," he used the stories and quotes he felt were the most important, combining the stories into a narrative that made sense for his situation and audience. Each Evangelist wrote from a particular perspective and for a specific audience. Therefore, each one gives us a slightly different view or interpretation of Jesus' life. Which one is true? Which one is the definitively inspired word of God? The answer is that they all are. Each Gospel is both true and inspired, yet each gives us a different aspect of the same person, mission and teachings. That is why we have four Gospels instead of one. We need a picture of Jesus that is as complete and accurate as possible—and just one narrative couldn't provide that.

This understanding, by the way, makes it imperative to avoid the temptation of taking short passages of Scripture out of context. People who do so find that they can justify just about anything they want by quoting particular passages from the Bible. But we must look at any passage of Scripture in the context of the rest of the Bible—and especially in light of Jesus' teachings. And we must always balance Jesus' words and actions in one Gospel with his words and actions in another.

With the knowledge we glean from biblical scholars, the insights of theologians, and the guidance of the magisterium (the teaching authority of the Church), we learn how to interpret Scripture in the light of the cultural and societal structures that existed in the era when particular biblical books were composed. Some directives in Scripture simply don't apply today. For instance, there are many rules and laws in Deuteronomy and Leviticus to which we Catholics do not adhere. We do not say, for example, that women are not to be touched during their time of menstruation, nor do we sprinkle the blood of sacrificed animals on the assembly as the ancient Hebrews did. Likewise, we allow marriage between people of differing faiths, even though that was forbidden when the Hebrews moved into their new land amidst people who worshiped other gods. And despite the fact that Saint Paul tells slaves that it is their duty in the Lord to obey their masters, we now know that slavery is a dehumanizing practice strongly opposed by the Church and by people of good will throughout the world.

Of course we now face many issues that simply didn't exist

in biblical times. For example, no one in those days could have imagined artificial birth control, much less *in vitro* fertilization or cloning. It is only through a continual process of theological investigation, prayer and discernment *in light of the Scriptures* that the Church forms teachings on the important issues and conflicts of our day.

Briefly Now...

Mark was the first to write his Gospel, and it is the shortest one. The Gospel of Mark doesn't contain any stories of Jesus' birth or childhood, so you won't find angels or shepherds, stars or a boyhood journey to the temple. Mark begins his story as Jesus is baptized as an adult.

Mark's Gospel is just as abrupt in its ending as in its beginning. There are no post-resurrection stories or ascensions or roads to Emmaus. Instead, Mark ends with the empty tomb and the command to "go tell the disciples." (In fact, some scholars believe that everything after verse sixteen of the final chapter was added by a later author to make the story seem more complete.)

Current biblical studies indicate that Mark wrote his Gospel about 65–70 a.d., during a time of great persecution of the Church. Two of its most important leaders, Peter and Paul, had just been martyred in Rome, and Mark's community was forced to grapple with the question of the cross. Why did Jesus and his followers have to die? Mark's answer was that Jesus is the Messiah not *in spite of* the cross but *because of* it. Suffering and the cross are instrumental parts of salvation. In fact, the cross is such a central aspect of Mark that this Gospel has sometimes been called a "Passion narrative with an extended introduction."

As you might guess, Mark wasn't one to elaborate or embellish his stories. He was all business, including only limited details and showing Jesus moving quickly from one event to another. His Gospel demonstrates the doubt, misunderstanding and fear of the disciples. These are the immediate visceral reactions that humans would be expected to have, and that indeed

41

we ourselves have, when confronted with Jesus. Yet the Gospel of Mark is also full of faith, hope, and the promise that God will ultimately prevail.

The Next Versions

When Matthew and Luke wrote their Gospels— about ten years later—they used Mark's Gospel as one of their sources, along with other compilations and their own materials. Like Mark, they each intended to address questions based on their own experience and intended audience.

Matthew wrote primarily for Jews who had converted to Christianity. He reassured his readers that they were not abandoning their roots, that Jesus was the fulfillment of the Jewish covenant and the Messiah they had been awaiting. Yet because so many Jews were converting, enormous tension developed between the Jews and the Jewish Christians, until finally the Jewish leadership voted to treat Christians as outcasts. Matthew spoke harshly against the Jewish leaders (the Pharisees and the Sadducees), as he tried to help the emerging Christian community find its identity apart from Judaism.

Matthew's was the only Gospel to use the word *church*, and he focused a substantial amount of attention on the life of the community. In Matthew, Jesus wants us to serve each other, to follow him, and to carry out his mission, acting as responsible stewards who carry the Good News to the ends of the earth.

Luke was the most inclusive of the four writers. He emphasized Jesus' ministry among the outcast and marginalized, including women and all those who were excluded by society. He threw open the door of God's grace and salvation to the Gentiles (or non-Jews), many of whom became Christian. In Luke's Gospel, Jesus is a compassionate healer who emphasizes the necessity of overturning oppressive power structures and recognizing all people as children of God. Prayer is a powerful force in this Gospel, and Luke offers repeated stories about how Jesus went off to pray, especially before undertaking a difficult task or journey.

You can get hungry just reading Luke's Gospel—it seems

that Jesus is always eating or on his way to or from a meal. In Jesus' day, status was largely defined by the company you kept and the place you had at the table, yet Jesus had the audacity to eat with sinners, outcasts, the poor and the oppressed, and he called on his followers to do the same. It's no wonder that when he designed a way for us to remember him he came up with a simple meal—one to which all are welcome and at which all are equal in God's eyes.

A Little While down the Road...

Matthew, Mark and Luke are called the *synoptic Gospels*. The prefix *syn* means "same" and the word *optic* means "sight." These three gospel accounts "see" Jesus in much the "same" way—first as a human being and later, when his followers finally comprehend who he is, as the Son of God. John's Gospel, however, takes the opposite tack. In John's Gospel, Jesus is right away recognized as the divine Son of God, the "Word" who "became flesh and dwelt among us." John's portrayal of Jesus is almost otherworldly at times. For example, Jesus is able to read people's minds and knows exactly what is going to happen.

John's Gospel was not written until almost the end of the first century A.D. (or C.E. for "common era" as some now refer to it). This was some sixty-five years after Jesus died. John leaves out much of the activity and parables of the earlier Gospels and concentrates instead on long discourses of Jesus' teaching. He doesn't seem as concerned with providing word-for-word quotes as he is with getting across the meaning of the Master's teaching.

A friend of mine recently described a guided retreat she experienced more than ten years ago. "I enjoyed the retreat at the time and felt I had learned a great deal from my retreat director," she said, "but it wasn't until now, as I look back, that I realize the tremendous impact it had on me. Almost every decision I made was based on principles I learned at that retreat, and the words of my director have been my guiding light. In retrospect, I have to admit that the retreat changed my life and in many ways made me who I am today."

This experience was so profound that it took my friend years to assess its impact. Things that seemed inconsequential or unrelated at the time became clear and seamlessly interrelated later. It was only with time, growth and wisdom that she could understand much of what had occurred.

Similarly, because it had been so long since Jesus' life, death and resurrection, John could write with a different perspective—one looking back at significant events with the understanding that can only come from having pondered long and hard about them. John's Gospel is therefore a great deal more theological than the other three. He uses symbols extensively, and includes many stories—such as the Raising of Lazarus, the Man Born Blind, and the Woman at the Well—that are found only in his Gospel.

What's a Church to Do?

With all these different versions of Jesus' life, what is the best and most complete way to tell the story at Mass? Should we combine them together, reading sections from each Gospel every year? Focus on just one Gospel and include others only when they contain unique information? Read each of the four in their entirety, one after the other? And what do we do with other biblical readings? Do we have one, two, three or more at each Mass? How can they best illuminate the Gospel reading?

This dilemma is compounded by the fact that these readings are the inspired word of God and that the Scripture stories proclaimed at Mass become the common language and shared experience of the members of the Church. For many, the readings at Mass are the only Scripture they ever hear. Decisions on choosing, compiling and proclaiming the various parts of the Bible at Mass, therefore, have enormous implications.

To resolve the problem for the Church, a group of scholars, theologians and bishops were given the task of compiling a book called the *Lectionary for Mass,* containing all the Scripture passages to be proclaimed at Mass. Although it is often said that the best way to kill an idea is to give it to a committee, this group produced an impressive result. The Lectionary, completed in English in 1970 and revised in 1998, is so well-respected that other Christian denominations have adopted it for their own use. This means that if you attend services at a Lutheran, Episcopalian or other mainline Protestant church, you will often hear the same Scripture readings you would have heard in your Catholic parish that Sunday.

A Compelling Series

Have you ever gone to a three-hour movie and felt that it went by in a flash, leaving you eager for the sequel? Or have you read a series of books so captivating that when you closed the cover of one volume you could hardly wait to open the next? Great stories take a long time to tell. Even though we hear about Jesus' birth, life, death and resurrection every year, it takes three whole years to tell the story completely.

Our Catholic Sunday Lectionary is organized into a three-year cycle, with each year prominently featuring a different Gospel. Year A is the year of Matthew; Year B concentrates on Mark; and Year C is Luke. The Gospel of John is interspersed throughout the other three and is also highlighted during Triduum. (When you celebrate Mass over the next few Sundays, listen to which Gospel is proclaimed and you will likely be able to determine the year, or cycle, the Church is in at the time.)

There are several reasons for including John within the other years. The first reason simply has to do with length. As already stated, Mark's Gospel is very short—so short that it would be difficult to section it into enough readings to cover an entire year. It would be like stretching a rubber band around a box that is too big for it. So more of John's Gospel is included during Year B than in the other two years. For instance, in Year B there is a section of five weeks in the middle of Ordinary Time when we hear the "bread of life" discourse from John's Gospel, in which Jesus explains that he is the living bread come down from heaven.

Another reason John is interspersed with the other three Gospels is to provide us with a complete picture of Jesus. While we need Matthew, Mark and Luke's perspective on Jesus as truly human, we also need John's understanding of Jesus as the eternal Word of God. We need to hear the events and parables of Jesus' life found in the synoptics, but we also need to hear Jesus' extended teachings found in John. Catholics believe that Jesus is both human and divine. If we are to keep these two realities in balance, we need to hear both at Mass throughout the year.

Day by Day

The Lectionary for days during the week is set up differently from the Sunday Lectionary. Weekday liturgies include only the first reading, a psalm, and then the Gospel reading. The first reading and the psalm are on a two-year cycle (Series I for odd years and Series II for even years), while the Gospels are presented in a single one-year series. Because these cycles are shorter, it may seem like less Scripture is covered during the week. But remember that there are six weekdays for every one Sunday. So in actual practice, there are twice as many different weekday Gospel readings over a one-year period as there are in the three-year Sunday cycle. Likewise, there are four times as many different weekday first readings in its two-year cycle as there are in the three-year Sunday cycle.

Feeding on the Scriptures

In the course of the three-year Sunday cycle, then, the assembly hears readings from almost every book in the Bible. There are substantial sections from some books, especially the epistles and the Gospels. Collectively, these readings form a sort of scriptural buffet, in which a person who carefully attends to the Word when it is proclaimed at Mass will be fed a varied and fairly complete fare.

Sometimes the readings comfort us, reassuring us of God's presence, care and saving power. Sometimes they challenge us, reversing our expectations and making us squirm in our seats. They remind us of our roots, our history, and our identity as a chosen people of God and baptized members of Christ's Body. They give us vision and mission, calling us beyond our complacency to live as true disciples. Perhaps most importantly, they give us hope. We know how faithful God has been in the past, we believe God is with us at every moment, and we trust that God's reign will ultimately prevail in heaven and on earth.

These are the words of life. Our challenge is to take the sustaining nourishment of the Scriptures, combine it with the life-giving nourishment of the table, and go forth to live a life of true discipleship and faithfulness in the world.

Questions for Reflection and Discussion

1. Some Christian denominations teach biblical fundamentalism, in which every word of Scripture is approached as absolute, historical fact. How does your understanding of Scripture agree or disagree with that view?

2. It is common for two or more people to attend an event together yet come away with very different impressions and reports of that event. Give an example of a time when you have experienced this. How did hearing other versions of the event change your own perspective?

3. How important is the Bible in your faith life? Is there any improvement you would like to make in your understanding or use of Scripture? What can you do to effect those changes?

4. Which of the four Evangelists is your favorite? Why?

5. The Scriptures often confront us, turning our concept of the world upside down or challenging us to change our lives. When was the last time a Scripture reading at Mass made you uncomfortable? Why? What did you do about it?

Chapter Four

Smells and Bells

We Catholics are a "sacramental" people. We believe that God's grace is mediated to us not only through the Bible but also through the material "stuff" of this world. We believe that we communicate with God, and God with us, by many and varied pathways. We believe that God is incarnate in the world around us and that all creation is permeated with the power and glory of God. In the ordinary, we see the extraordinary. In the midst of earth, we see heaven. In finite humanity, we see infinite divinity. All of creation is sacred to us because it is a visible expression of the invisible transcendent reality. Because we are a sacramental people, we surround ourselves with symbols and signs, sacraments and sacramentals that connect us to our faith in the incarnate God.

So What Is a Symbol?

A symbol is a means by which an interior or spiritual quality can be expressed in the exterior and material world. In other words, we take things we cannot see, feel, hear, taste or touch and make them tangible through symbols. The symbol is not determined by arbitrary designation, however; it can function as a symbol only when it points to another reality and also participates in the reality to which it points.

The nature of a symbol is much easier to illustrate with examples than with words. Think, for instance, about the characteristics of water. Water quenches our thirst, nourishes the earth, and washes our bodies and clothes—and water is great fun for playing and splashing around. Just being near a body of water often connects us with something deep in the human psyche. It is renewing, invigorating, mysterious and wonderful. I remember hot summer days when my throat felt parched, and the mere sight of a water fountain made me yearn for that cool, refreshing stream. When I was finally able to drink, it seemed there was nothing better in the world. The human race could not survive without water.

In our faith, water is a symbol of life. In other words, the concept of life is made tangible in water. It is not arbitrary, though. Water can be a powerful and effective symbol of life because it participates in the reality to which it points; it actually does give life.

There is also a shadow side to water. Have you ever been caught in a flood? Has someone you loved died by drowning? Have you seen or been affected by a mudslide caused by torrential rains? If so, then you know firsthand the dangerous and death-dealing force of water.

In our faith, water is also a symbol of death. Living and dying are intimately joined together in one mystery. Therefore, when we plunge people into the waters of baptism to "die to sin," we are aware that if we hold them under the water too long they will quite literally die. Instead, we bring them up, sputtering and spattering and full of the new life that is theirs in Christ.

Now envision a traffic signal. Everyone knows the red circle on a traffic signal means "stop." Is this a symbol? No, it is not. Although the light points to a different reality, it does not participate in it. There is nothing about red-ness that participates in stop-ness. It could just as easily be any other color, including purple with pink polka dots. The red light is an arbitrary designation decided by the creators of the traffic signal and agreed upon by our society.

Indeed, psychologists assert that red in the human psyche is the color of anger and passion and energy. Thus, red has a lot more to do with "go" than it does with "stop." Still, because our society has agreed and has written laws designating that red means "stop," that is the meaning it has for us. It is a sign, but it is not a symbol.

But It Doesn't *Do* Anything

Because it is an arbitrary designation, the meaning of a sign is clearly defined and is precisely what we say it is. The meaning of a symbol, however, is deep, complex and nuanced for each experience and in each person, defying easy explanation.

Symbols are gratuitous. They are not "useful" or productive. For example, we don't eat birthday cake for its nutritional value. We don't light the Easter fire because we need to burn something. We don't put ashes on our foreheads because the grit helps our looks. We don't get full by eating the Eucharistic meal.

People who are uncomfortable with gray areas, who want things scientifically exact, have difficulty with symbols. For them, flowers are simply a group of plants, not an expression of love, life or budding growth. We have to learn to see and appreciate symbols.

Water, Water Everywhere

Let's return to our example of water. Notice how often we use water when we celebrate Mass:

The font: In the architecture of many newly built or redesigned church buildings, a large baptismal font is a prominent feature at the entrance to the worship space. Older churches have small holy water fonts at the entrance doors. The fonts symbolize that the liturgy is our right and our duty by virtue of baptism, that we are joined into one Body with the other members of the community through baptism, and that we are incorporated into the mission of Jesus through baptism. So every time we enter the church to celebrate Mass, we are invited to sign ourselves with water. We accept once again our identity as Christians by making the sign of the cross on our bodies, using water blessed by the priest and coming from the same source as the water for baptizing new members. While we often do this gesture without thinking, it has deep significance and power for those who carefully attend to it.

The sprinkling rite: There are many liturgies, especially during the Easter season, when we participate in a sprinkling rite. Using an *aspergillum*, a device with a metallic rod and rounded end that soaks up water, the priest can send sprinkles of water through the assembly with a flick of the wrist. Many parishes have replaced the aspergillum with branches and sprinkling bowls, allowing many ministers to sprinkle water through the assembly simultaneously. The intent is for the water to rain down upon the assembly, reminding us again of our baptism and our life in Christ.

Liturgy: During the Preparation of the Gifts, a small amount of water is mixed with the wine. In the biblical stories of the crucifixion, we hear that blood and water flowed forth from Jesus' side. The blood and water signify the human and the divine, life and death, joined together and offered to God. After the Preparation of the Gifts, the presiding priest washes his hands. In the early Church it was necessary to wash one's hands after receiving all the gifts people brought from their homes. The gesture now expresses a desire for inward purification, as the priest prays to the Lord to "wash away my iniquities; cleanse me from my sin."

The Light of the World

With the advent of electricity, it is no longer necessary to rely on fire as a source of light. Of course, when the electricity goes out, a lighted candle is a welcome sight. And if you are returning to a campsite at night, you know the palpable feeling of relief and gratitude when you catch a glimpse of the campfire through the trees. It is at such times that we truly appreciate the biblical image of Jesus as the light shining in the darkness.

Our experience of fire goes beyond our need for illumination, however. Have you ever sat in front of a fireplace or a bonfire and been mesmerized by the flames, drawn into the mystery as they flicker and lick the air? Fire is a powerful and mysterious force, drawing us into itself like the breath of God. We marvel as each candle is slowly consumed, giving its substance for our benefit. We are well aware of our dependency on fire for warmth, cooking and comfort.

We also know that fire can rage out of our control, consuming millions of acres of forest, reducing entire homes to smoldering heaps of ash, and destroying everything in its path. It is a force to be feared as well as befriended. We stand in awe and yet we are fascinated. Fire possesses a might we do not understand. Although we can get close to it, and indeed we long to be close to it, we can't quite touch it. It is beyond us, yet within our reach at the same time.

All these factors come into play as we light the candles of liturgy or ignite the flame of the paschal candle at the Easter Vigil. We proclaim Christ as the Light of the World, the One who dispels our darkness and calls us into the divine. We are captivated by the flames, drawn deep into the power and hypnotic mystery of God. We surround ourselves with the ambiguity of the symbol, with the power of life and death, the transcendent mystery, the mesmerizing force before which we kneel and to which we cling.

The Oil of Gladness

Have you watched those wrestling extravaganzas on TV? Or have you seen a bodybuilding competition? For each of these events, the competitors want to project a healthy, vital glow, illustrating their attractiveness, their strength, and their raw beauty. To achieve this effect, they slather themselves with oil.

Have you looked at the list of ingredients for the lotions and ointments you use every day? Most of them are based in oil. Have your hands or face been so dry they felt like sandpaper or you imagined them splitting open? Do you remember the soothing feeling of an oily lotion sinking into the cracks and pores, soothing your skin and nourishing it back to life?

Have you ever given an expensive lotion to someone? You would not have given such a gift to just anyone, of course. It would be a person quite special for whom you wanted to show your love, respect and honor.

From the time of antiquity, oil has been used in religious rituals and for the anointing of priests, prophets and kings. In fact, the word *messiah* means "the anointed one." Anointing or "Christ-ening" indicates divine election for specific tasks.

Oil is a marvelous symbol because of the many connections we have with oils in our everyday life. (I am not speaking, of course, of motor oil. Although it lubricates our cars and provides the means for engines to propel us down the road, I don't know many people who would want to have it soak into their skin.)

There are three blessed oils used in the Catholic Church: the oil of the catechumens, chrism, and the oil of the sick. All three are basically olive oil, although chrism is perfumed with balsam. These oils are blessed by the bishop at the Chrism Mass, celebrated every year at the beginning of Holy Week. Each parish is then given the amount of oil they need for the coming twelve months.

When oil is used to anoint the sick, its soothing nature reflects the healing for which we pray. As people are anointed in preparation for baptism, the oil of the catechumens symbolizes the wisdom and strength necessary to approach the living waters. In baptism, confirmation, ordination of priests and consecration of altars, the sweet fragrance of chrism combines with the life-giving nature of oil to sanctify those anointed in the midst of the community. In all cases, oil signifies respect, honor, divine favor, and health in mind, body and spirit.

Life Needs the Real Thing

In most worship spaces there is an array of flowers and plants. While they serve to beautify our space, they are not present simply for decoration. Rather, their symbolism expresses deep human realities.

On a gut level, most people connect with plants. Simply

having a vase of flowers on the kitchen table brightens my day. Giving live plants and flowers to others can convey love, sorrow, regret or kindness.

Plants and flowers are powerfully symbolic because they so closely relate to us. Live plants are sometimes messy, like our lives. The dirt can spill and some of the leaves may die. They often need to be cut back or pruned in order to grow well—just as we do. They need constant nurturing and care, like our faith and our souls. Some plants are incredibly hardy, even surviving neglect; others are quite fragile, requiring a great deal of attention in order to flourish. Similarly, there are people who seem unusually strong and others who need a great deal of attention. Many plants and flowers go into a dormant stage, where we might swear they are dead. Beneath the surface, however, change and growth are happening—life that is not readily apparent on the surface is preparing to emerge through the soil. In a similar pattern, human beings often withdraw from their routines, especially in times of grief or difficulty, only to emerge with a renewed sense of life and purpose.

Allow me to express one personal pet peeve here. It is tempting for many parishes to forego the mess, the necessary care, and the replacement expense of live plants by buying sets of artificial plants. This also applies to candles, as some parishes use electric candles rather than wax ones. Yet, all of these symbolic connections are lost if the plants or candles are plastic or artificial. These do not draw us into transcendent mystery, into realities beyond ourselves. It is impossible to symbolize life with something that only pretends to be alive. Artificial plants and candles reflect sterility and convenience at the expense of deeper and more profound meaning. Please try to use the "real thing" in your liturgies, prayer services, and formation sessions.

We Need a Lighthouse in Here

One of our great liturgical symbols, incense, has created a lot of controversy, primarily because of its overuse. People (especially those with allergies or asthma) have too often been forced out of the worship space amid billowing, overly perfumed clouds of incense. The intent of incense is not to create a fog or to restrict airways. Rather, when we use quickly dispersing, lighter scents of non-allergenic incense, it can be a powerful and prayerful experience.

Smells are carriers of memory. Whenever I smell lilacs, for example, I am transported back to my childhood, when I climbed trees and played regularly in my grandmother's yard. In the spring, the sweet aroma of the lilac bushes that lined her lot was intoxicating. I remember burying my face in the blossoms, filling my lungs with what I deemed the fragrance of heaven.

Likewise, when I smell incense I remember the awe of solemn ritual under the soaring arches of the Basilica of St. Francis Xavier. I remember the sadness of funerals for loved ones no longer physically with us. I remember the mystery of Benediction and kneeling in humble adoration. I remember the wonder of sacred spaces, times and people, and the desire to be close to this mysterious God who came to dwell among us.

Incense signifies respect, reverence and prayer. Incensing the book of prayer or the people who are gathered to pray is like anointing them with perfume, indicating their precious and holy nature, while the smoke creates an aura of mystery and transcendence. We experience our pleasing fragrance before God, and we see and feel our prayers rising on the clouds of heaven. Then, as the incense permeates the entire room, we know that the unseen God fills the space all around us, enveloping us with comfort and love. Properly used, incense is a visible and dramatic means of connecting us to the divine.

Words Are Inadequate

Water, fire, oil, flowers and incense are only some of the major symbols of our faith. They form part of the language of the Mass, a symbolic language with which we sometimes struggle in a world oriented to efficiency, production and precision.

Some people are tempted to dismiss the significance of symbols by saying, "Oh, it's only a symbol—not the real thing." Yet, symbols are sometimes the most "real" things we have.

Symbols recognize there is a deeper, unseen reality, one that is actually more real than all those things to which we commonly assign reality. Symbols hold a range of meanings within themselves, a depth and ambiguity able to contain tension and paradox. Symbols alone are capable of taking over when mere words are not enough.

Think of a kiss between lovers. It is a symbol of their love, yet it also participates in that love. It is absolutely "real," with a meaning going beyond words—and, in fact, its meaning cannot be adequately expressed in any other way. So it is with the symbols of faith. When we are immersed in water, when we are anointed with the fragrant oil, when we behold flowers bursting forth or flames flickering in the darkness or incense rising to the heavens, the experience goes beyond words. In and through symbols, we truly encounter the divine.

Questions for Reflection and Discussion

1. We use many symbols in our everyday lives, from wedding rings to the national flag. What are some of the favorite symbols in your life? Why are they significant to you?

2. Imagine two baptismal celebrations. In one, water is poured over the child's head. In the other, the child is undressed and totally immersed in the water. What differences do you see in the meaning of the two symbols?

3. Describe a time when you were given a bouquet of fresh flowers. How did the flowers smell? How did they look and feel? What did they signify about your relationship with the giver?

4. Do you have a cross or a crucifix hanging in your home or workplace? Why or why not? Why do you think it is important to have a cross or crucifix prominent in our worship space?

5. Some people keep blessed water at the door of their home, light candles when their family gathers for mealtime, and make the sign of the cross with oil on each other's hands or foreheads to mark special occasions. What symbols of the faith do you use in your home? In what ways could you include symbols of the faith more often?

Chapter Five

So Where Is Christ, Anyway?

How many ways can you be present if you aren't physically there? I remember a memorial service at which some friends gathered to recall a friend who had died. Somehow, whenever another person entered the room, our friend's presence grew until it felt as if she were sitting among us.

At that gathering, we read some letters that our friend had written to various members of our group, especially as she was dying. We could all imagine her voice and just how she would have said each phrase. In the reading of those letters, our friend's words came to life as if she were speaking directly to us.

Before she died, our friend made small pieces of tapestry as memorials for each of us. After we read her letters, one member of the group silently walked around the room and gave each of us our own piece of tapestry. There was no explanation of each piece or description of how they fit together. There didn't need to be. Our friend's love for us was only slightly more tangible than our connection to one another in that love.

Finally, we sang songs of joy and hope, of comfort and healing. And we knew that our friend was singing with us, hugging us as the tears washed down our faces. In many and varied ways, she was present even though she wasn't physically there.

In similar fashion, although Jesus is no longer physically here on earth, Christ is really and truly present at Mass in many forms. The Catholic Church teaches that there are at least four ways in which we experience the tangible presence of Christ when we celebrate liturgy: in the community that gathers for the celebration; in the ministers who lead us in prayer and worship; in the words of Scripture; and in the consecrated elements that become Christ's body and blood.

The Gathered Assembly

Just as those of us who gathered for the memorial service carried our friend's spirit, each of us at Mass carries Christ in our hearts, minds and souls. Jesus taught that wherever two or three are gathered in his name, he is there. Every person who enters the worship space makes the presence of Christ more keenly felt, because Christ is enfleshed in us.

The presence of Christ in the people is essential. For Mass to be truly "celebrated," it isn't sufficient just to have a priest; there has to be an assembly as well. And it cannot be a disinterested assembly, such as might occur at a bus stop or in a movie theater. In those circumstances we are individuals who happen to be in the same place at the same time, but there is no felt connection between us, nor is there any activity expected of us.

If we are to fully "celebrate" Mass, we cannot simply be there by chance or by habit or even out of duty. We have to reach out to one another, to join our hearts and hands, to recognize our interdependence on one another and our ultimate dependence on God, and to be wholeheartedly involved in the experience. Even in times of personal sadness or difficulty, when it seems we have little left to give the community, we give what we have and that is enough. The phrase used in official Church documents is "full, conscious, active participation." Mass is not meant to be a spectator event, a performance that you can sleep through or a duty to be endured in order to "put in your time."

An Emerging Understanding

There have been periods in the history of the Church when the assembly was expected to be non-communicative and passive. People talked about "going to" or "attending" Mass rather than "celebrating" Mass. Children were taught that it was a sin to look around at other people during the liturgy, because that distracted from the central focus of actions and prayers at the altar. Prayer books for the Mass often described what was happening but did not encourage people to participate. I remember my mother and other family members bringing rosaries or other prayer aids to Mass in order to feel that they had actually spent their time "praying."

Prompted by the liturgical reforms of the twentieth century and the documents of the Second Vatican Council, however, we have recovered a sense of the liturgy that dates back to the early Church. The disciples of Christ believed that their gathering was the most important symbol and sacrament of their faith. They believed each person was essential to the Body of Christ and that it was the right and duty of everyone present to participate fully in the ritual. In fact, the word *liturgy* comes from the Greek word *leitourgia*, which literally means "the work of the people." We are a chosen people, a holy people, a people founded on Christ and joined by faith, called to celebrate and to be sent back out into the world. When we assemble at Mass, we are truly the presence of Christ.

The Ministers

I once went sailing on a large boat and was amazed at how many people were involved in the process and yet how smoothly the navigation went. Each person had a function. Some were more visible than others, but in order for us to arrive safely at our destination everyone had to work together in seamless harmony.

Each person at Mass is a minister called to participate fully and completely in the liturgy. Yet to maintain our bearings and avoid chaos, some members of the assembly take visible roles, leading the prayer and singing, proclaiming the Scriptures, and serving the needs of those gathered. Each visible minister, while no more important that the rest of the assembly, is a means by which Christ is present at Mass.

In the liturgy, the priest stands *in persona Christi,* which means "in the person of Christ." This does not mean that the priest abandons his humanity or becomes someone else. He still has all his gifts and charisms—and, to the chagrin of some members of the assembly, his human limitations as well. Yet ideally, he acts and proclaims in such a way that he points the assembly to the living presence of Christ in our midst.

The priest stands at the head of the assembly as presider. To *preside* literally means "to be seated in front of." The priest's role as presider takes two forms. First, like the host or hostess of a large gathering, the presider coordinates and controls the timing and flow of the different parts of the celebration, enabling the rhythm of the Mass to draw us nearer to the working of God. The presider forms the link between the various liturgical ministers and the assembly, harmonizing all the roles in such a way that the assembly can worship well.

Second, the presider acts as the one voice of the people. He gathers the prayers of the assembly and, on the community's behalf, offers their prayers to God. He usually is the one who breaks open the word of God in the homily, and he speaks aloud the Eucharistic Prayer, during which he consecrates the bread and wine that God transforms into the body and blood of Christ. Finally, he sends the assembly forth on their mission to live the liturgy in their daily lives.

As head of the ministering community and of the praying community, the priest fulfills his overarching role, which is to embody and model the presence of the risen Christ. He speaks authoritatively for Christ, offering words of absolution, voicing Jesus' own words at the Last Supper, and declaring that the Lamb of God is indeed in our midst.

The Word

All Christian denominations agree that the Scriptures are the inspired word of God and that Christ is truly present in that living word. We are a people who live by a book we have carried with us through the ages, from generation to generation, through time and place. We are a people hungry and thirsty for God, whose word is food and drink for our souls. In the Scriptures, God speaks directly to us, touches us, challenges us and heals us.

The readings in the Bible are proclaimed everywhere and anywhere that Catholic people gather to pray. The Catholic

Church goes so far as to declare that when the Scriptures are proclaimed in the assembly it is Christ himself who speaks. Therefore, the Liturgy of the Word deserves its special prominence in the liturgical celebration.

The Church calls the Liturgy of the Word the foundation of the Mass and the foundation of our lives. Remember, a *foundation* is the bedrock that holds up a house; if a tornado blows a building off its base, the entire structure will collapse. We would do well, then, to listen carefully and attentively, using the words we hear as building blocks to fashion a strong foundation for our faith.

The Scripture readings are multi-faceted. They remind us of our history, recalling the stories of God's interaction with humankind. By remembering what has happened in the past, we reaffirm our identity as God's people. Yet, the readings are not only about events that happened thousands of years ago; they also bring those lessons into the present, challenging us to live out our identity in today's world.

The Bible is a dangerous book if people listen to it and live by it. During times of persecution in the first few centuries after Jesus died, the Romans felt they could demoralize Christians by destroying what was most precious to them: the words that gave them life. Emperors and soldiers tried desperately to confiscate the holy texts and burn them. In those days, people literally risked their lives and were sometimes martyred for their attempts to protect the Scriptures from desecration or destruction.

Most of us, at least in this country, do not have to risk our lives to proclaim the word in the assembly today. Instead, we often take the Bible too much for granted. We must remember that it is the living word of God, and if that does not snap us out of our comfort zone and prompt us to continuous change and conversion, then we aren't really listening.

What Does It Mean?

For Catholics, interpreting Scripture is not done in a fundamentalist, literalist fashion. Rather, the Catholic Church teaches us to be *contextualists*. That is, we try to understand what the author and the community that gave birth to the passage were trying to communicate in their own time. Then we move forward to ask what that Scripture passage is saying to us today, in our time. We pay attention to the literary style, the underlying cultural beliefs, and the audience. We search for the different ways that God's word speaks to us, knowing that the Bible is timeless and authoritative, compellingly proclaimed and followed in many countries, cultures and circumstances across the world and over time.

In fact, this is part of the power of Scripture. Because it is God's inspired word, it has a depth and intricacy that never fades. It has the ability to speak to wealthy Americans and destitute Nigerians, to teenagers and octogenarians, to the successful and the unemployed, to the healthy and the dying. Although it was written thousands of years ago, its message, even today, remains life-giving and potent. We can hear a story repeated for years, yet each time we hear it we can receive a new insight. Sometime there is an aspect that suddenly leaps off the page, something we never noticed before. At other times, we hear a new message not because the *passage* is different, but because *we* are different.

When we attend closely to the Liturgy of the Word at Mass, we continually take God's word into ourselves. In so doing, we are challenged, convinced and transformed, becoming a beacon of God's love to all those we encounter. "The word of the Lord" has the power to change us and to strengthen our fledgling faith, molding us into the people we were created to be. We know that God is speaking to us, and we pray that our eyes, ears and hearts may be opened to the divine presence. We will be amazed at what we learn and the ways in which God can form us—individually and as a community. The proclaimed word is truly one of the ways Christ is present in the Mass.

The Consecrated Elements

On the night before he died, Jesus "took a loaf of bread, and after blessing it he broke it and gave it to his disciples, and said,

'Take, eat; this is my body.' Then he took a cup and after giving thanks he gave it to them, saying, 'Drink from it, all of you; for this is my blood of the covenant, which is poured out for many for the forgiveness of sins'" (Matthew 26:26–28). Jesus thus declared that bread and wine, common foods from earth and vine, become his body and blood in the Eucharistic meal.

In the Catholic Church this is called the "Real Presence." We believe that through the words of consecration in the Eucharistic Prayer and the action of the community, the bread and wine actually become the body and blood of Christ. Although the elements maintain their outward appearance, they are in reality transformed (or, in the term we inherited from Thomas Aquinas, *transubstantiated*) into the body and blood of Jesus Christ himself. They do not merely *represent* or *remind* us of Jesus' presence. They *are* his presence.

Since the consecrated elements are truly the presence of Christ, we must treat them with great respect and dignity. Leftover wine is consumed; leftover bread is reserved in a container called a *ciborium*. A small container called a *pyx* is used to carry consecrated bread to the sick and the homebound. The vessels are washed in a special sink called a *sacrarium*, so that any crumbs or drops go directly into the ground rather than into the sewer system.

O Come Let Us Adore

Many parishes practice Eucharistic Adoration, a devotion that emphasizes the Catholic belief in the Real Presence. A large consecrated host is placed in a container called a *monstrance* (from the Latin *monstrare*, the root of the word *demonstrate*, which literally means "to show"). The faithful then gather outside of Mass to pray in the presence of the body of Christ. This is a deeply spiritual practice that brings comfort and hope to many.

The Church cautions, however, that Eucharistic Adoration is never to become separated from the Eucharistic Liturgy itself. The central purpose of reserving consecrated bread is to serve the ill and the homebound; adoration and prayer are secondary benefits. Eucharistic Adoration is to flow into and out of the liturgy. For example, the consecrated host that is used for adoration comes from a community celebration of the liturgy, and after a period of time it is eaten by the community and replaced with another. Those concerned about attending to the body of Christ in the host must be equally concerned about attending to the Body of Christ in our world—the homeless, the poor, the imprisoned, and the "least of these."

By issuing these guidelines, the Church hopes to avoid misunderstandings caused by oversensitivity to the sacredness of the elements. There was an extended period of time in Catholic history, for instance, in which the unworthiness and sinfulness of the laity was stressed so highly that few people dared receive Communion. They felt that in order to receive the body and blood of Christ they had to be absolutely pure and sinless. In fact, at one point the Church made it mandatory to receive Communion at Easter time so the faithful would be sure to come to the table at least once a year.

When people did receive Communion, they often did so at a side altar, before or after Mass, rather than approaching the altar during the liturgy. They were not considered worthy to touch the consecrated bread or drink the consecrated wine. The priest placed the host on the outstretched tongue of the recipient, and the cup never left the altar.

Current liturgical documents make it clear that Jesus' intention was for all to come to the table. We are to eat and drink in his memory, not because we can ever be worthy but because Christ invites—in fact commands—us to do so. We are also invited to follow Jesus' directives literally by taking the host in our hands to eat and taking the cup to drink. After over two thousand years, the invitation to the table stands. The Real Presence of Christ is our food and drink for the journey, strengthening and challenging us to become what we receive. Liturgy and life are one.

Mix and Blend

These four ways in which Christ is present—within the gathered community, in the ministers, in the proclaimed word, and in the consecrated elements—are not as distinct as such a list makes them appear. In fact, any division is artificial, since they are not actually separate at all; it is the Holy Spirit that binds them together. It is the Spirit that breathes Christ into the Church. It is through the Spirit that the members of the assembly become, in the words of theology professor Stephen Schmidt, "twice-birthed, watered-wet little Christs" at baptism. The Spirit enlivens gifts of service and gives the power to embody Christ in the sacrament of Holy Orders. The Spirit inspired the written word, and it is through the inspiration of the Spirit that Christ himself proclaims the word in the assembly. The food of the Eucharist is transformed into Christ by the invocation of the Spirit. In the Mass, the presence of Christ flows through, among and around the entire celebration, infusing us with the Spirit, showering us with grace and leading us on to authentic discipleship. Everywhere we look, whether at the table, at the ambo, or in the pew next to us, we see Christ.

This encompassing presence is both comforting and unsettling. When we believe that Christ is truly present, it changes us. A friend of mine who is a priest often says that if Catholics truly believed Christ himself is present in all the ways we profess, we could not stop the stampede of people crowding into Mass at every opportunity. Where else can we experience God so profoundly or in so many ways? Where else can we receive the nourishment for which our souls hunger and thirst? Where else can we practice what we are to be living every day in the world—being Christ, proclaiming the kingdom, ministering to the poor and to one another, eating and drinking in unity and equality with everyone?

Once we believe in Christ present, we can no longer sit passively and let the priest "say" the Mass for us. Our ears are opened to the challenging words of Scripture. We follow the irresistible urge to join our voices as one in prayer and song. We reach out to one another in compassion, love and devotion. We come to the table to take into our own bodies the actual flesh of Christ. We bare our yearning hearts and are filled with the peace and grace that only God can give. There is nothing like this experience anywhere else on earth.

Questions for Discussion and Reflection

1. When were you aware of the presence of someone who was not physically there? Remember and describe the experience.

2. In what ways are you most aware of the presence of Christ during the Mass? How do you think of Christ as being present to you as an individual? To the entire community?

3. What connections do you see between the practice of Eucharistic Adoration and the work of social justice in the world?

4. Think about your own language concerning the Mass. Do you say that you "go to" Mass, "attend" Mass, "celebrate" Mass—or do you use another word? Do you refer to the priest as "saying" Mass, "celebrating" Mass, or "presiding" at Mass? How does your word choice affect your experience of and participation in the Mass?

5. Describe a time when you changed something you did during the week based on your encounter with Christ at Mass.

Chapter Six

Moving, Praying and Singing

When we eat a family meal together, we sit down. When we sing the national anthem, we all stand and place our hands on our hearts. It is natural for us to express our inner attitudes by the outward posture of our bodies. The posture gives meaning to the moment, and the moment gives meaning to the posture.

Granted, the meaning we assign to body postures is somewhat arbitrary. In another culture, another faith or another generation, various postures could be interpreted quite differently. A proper posture of greeting, for example, could vary from a polite bow to a handshake to an enthusiastic embrace with a kiss on both cheeks.

The ambiguity of meaning is not totally erased even in liturgical circles. For instance, liturgists and theologians disagree about the proper posture for the Eucharistic Prayer: Should we stand or should we kneel? Still, there are some commonalities of meaning that help make sense of the different body postures we assume during the Mass.

Will You Please Sit Down?

Sitting conveys an attitude of listening, meditation and contemplation. It is a posture of rest and of receiving. When someone has important news for you, they often tell you to sit down. Audiences sit for a speech, and students sit for a lecture. The recommended posture for contemplative prayer is sitting with both feet on the ground.

We sit at Mass to hear the important "news" of the word of God in the first two readings and the psalm. We sit in silence between the readings and after Communion, to meditate on the mysteries being revealed. During the homily, we sit as the

Scriptures are broken open for us.

We never sit for too long, however, because we are not a passive audience. We are not sitting as if in front of the TV waiting to be entertained. We sit during Mass to listen fully to the Scriptures or to let the silence wash over us as we take the message deeper into our hearts. As we "receive" the word, however, we remain an active assembly of celebrants wholeheartedly engaged and invested in the action of the liturgy, so that God can use the liturgy to transform us in our daily lives.

Stand on Your Own Two Feet

We stand to greet others, especially if we intend to show deference and respect. For instance, we stand when the president enters the room or when a judge approaches the bench. When a speaker or performer has done an outstanding job, we honor that person with a standing ovation. Standing is a posture of dignity, as we are reminded by the phrase, "standing on your own two feet." We "stand up" to be counted, and we "stand for" something when we believe in it. Standing is also an active posture, readying us for movement or response.

At Mass, we stand during the Introductory Rites, welcoming one another respectfully and warmly, preparing ourselves to celebrate the ritual. We stand to honor the proclamation of the Gospel and to profess the Creed. We stand during portions of the Eucharistic Prayer, when we pray in the words Jesus gave us, and in preparation for our dismissal into the world.

A related activity, with layers of purpose and meaning, is the act of walking. When we walk, we sometimes move from one place to another very directly, taking the shortest pathway or a pre-planned, timed route. At other times, a circuitous journey can be delightful—taking a side trip to chat with a friend, following the random path of a butterfly, or simply slowing down to appreciate the meaning of the journey.

Walking in procession is an integral part of the Mass. We begin with movement, as ministers process into the midst of the assembly. *The Book of the Gospels* is processed to the ambo. The gifts are processed through the people to be placed on the altar. The entire community processes to the table to be fed, remembering that we are on a journey to the heavenly banquet for which we now rehearse. Finally, we process out from our place of celebration into the wider community to take the liturgy into the world. Each of these movements is an act of prayer, done with beauty and spirit, reminding us that we are the chosen people of a God in whom we "live and move and have our being."

We Kneel before Thee

When I was a young child, my family would gather in the living room to pray the rosary. Despite the fact that chairs and comfortable couches begged us to sit, every one of us knelt for the prayer. We were taught to kneel beside our beds for bedtime prayer, and I occasionally caught a glimpse of my mother kneeling in prayer when she thought she was alone. Pictures in my prayer book depicted people kneeling in adoration or petition. In art and in practice, kneeling is the body position most commonly associated with prayer.

Genuflection is a variation of kneeling, in which we go down on one knee as an act of homage before the Blessed Sacrament. Bowing, either by inclining one's head forward or by bending over from the waist, signifies much the same reverential attitude as kneeling.

The meaning of prayerful kneeling comes from the posture's long human history. Kings and governmental authorities often demanded that subjects kneel in their presence to recognize their superiority or even their claims to divinity. In fact, early Christians were martyred for refusing to kneel in homage before the emperor. Defendants in court used to kneel before the judge to beg for mercy. Pilgrims sometimes "walk" on their knees in sorrow and humility along the path of Christ's passion. Traditionally, a man kneels before a woman when he proposes marriage.

We need to know what it feels like and what it means to be a people on our knees, whether in penitence, sorrow, humility, respect or deference. Again, although kneeling can lead us into

71

private individual prayer, that is not its purpose in the liturgy. When we all kneel as one body, we express most profoundly that we are creatures before our Creator—sinful, repentant and broken, but trusting that we shall be saved, forgiven and healed.

Raise Your Hands, Please

When we pray privately, we frequently place our hands together in some fashion, with palms flat against each other and fingers either pointed upward or clasped around one another. We often close our eyes and bow our heads as well, adopting a posture of introspection. Try it, and become aware of how it feels for you to be in this body position. Most people say it feels safe, private, interior, individual, comfortable and secure. You can be totally unaware of what people around you are doing when you are in this position and center yourself on the God who dwells within your heart.

In liturgical prayer, however, we are encouraged to adopt an ancient position of prayer from the early Church called the *orans* position. In fact, there are drawings in the catacombs of St. Priscilla in Rome depicting early Christians praying in the *orans* position as early as the second century. Reminiscent of Christ on the cross, it is an open-armed posture, with head raised and hands either lifted upwards toward the heavens or outward toward the community. The *orans* position is the most frequent posture of prayer used by the presider at Mass.

When I ask people to adopt the *orans* position and tell me how it feels, they say it is open, vulnerable, communal, scary and surrendering. You are totally aware of what people around you are doing. Rather than having an inward attitude, you are focused on the God who dwells in all of us, the God to whom we offer everything we are—not just as an individual, but also as a community.

That is precisely why the *orans* position is such a good one for liturgical prayer. At Mass we are a community, a body joined together as one, surrendering and opening ourselves to God. While there are moments in the Mass for silent reflection, the liturgy is not primarily a time of private, individual prayer. Private prayer should be happening all week, preparing us for the liturgy. Mass is a time of communal prayer, singing with one voice, responding with one heart, and praising with one soul.

Dance of the Heart

At our liturgies, there are always young children who just can't hold still when the music starts. They bounce and dance, sometimes escaping their parents and running into the aisles as they move in complete freedom to the rhythm. The assembly usually smiles on these young cherubs, and I have experienced a tinge of jealousy at the lack of self-consciousness in their whole-body prayer.

In the Hebrew Scriptures, dance was integral to worship. Men and women from Miriam to David danced before the Lord in praise and thanksgiving. In ancient tribal cultures, too, prayer was danced to express veneration, supplication and joy. Currently, dance is very much a part of religious worship in Asia, Africa and the Middle East, as well as in Native American, Hispanic and African-American communities. Unfortunately, Western and European cultures seem to have lost that connection. "Dance" in the Euro-American world is something that couples do at a wedding or well-rehearsed ensembles do in the theater.

In actuality, the liturgical postures we've already discussed form a kind of dance. We move our bodies in ordered and synchronized ways throughout the liturgy, affecting the nature and meaning of our prayer and helping to make the invisible community visible. Some communities incorporate other ritual movements as well. For instance, a liturgical dancer may lead the assembly in a hand gesture during the psalm or as a response to the intercessions. Or there may be a dance in responsorial form, where the dancer prays a verse of a song with movement and the assembly joins in with movement on the chorus. The intent is to engage the whole person and to help the words of hymns, songs and psalms come alive.

Interpretation of Scripture is another role for liturgical

dance. Often, a Scripture reading can be better understood by combining the verbal reading with non-verbal actions. The choreography is thoughtfully designed to highlight the words and meaning of Scripture, drawing the assembly into a fuller understanding of God's word.

The dance or movement is well done when it helps the community to understand that God remembers them, loves them, and calls them. Although the dancers must be competent, liturgical dance is never intended as a performance; rather, it is supposed to be a form of prayer. Although there may be solo parts in a particular movement (just as a cantor may sing verses alone), the dance should never be a solo act; it should draw the entire assembly into the meaning of the prayer. Liturgical dance is an extension of the movements we already incorporate in the Mass, deepening the praying experience and involving our bodies in the rhythm and flow of our praise, repentance, petition or thanksgiving.

Rise Up Singing

Music has the power to go beyond words, to express what is otherwise inexpressible, to bring disparate people together, and to carry memories and emotions. When I was so deeply in grief that words failed, music held my broken heart. Music is sometimes called "the language of love," articulating the depth of one's devotion to another. Anthems unite nations, the folk song "We Shall Overcome" unites generations of civil rights activists, and the playing of taps binds the hearts of veterans across the decades. Certain songs or melodies immediately transport me back to my childhood or my high school days, eliciting feelings of sorrow, joy or peace that I associate with those times.

Early philosophers like Plato believed music could permanently alter a person's character. At various times in history, forms of music have been banned for their potentially negative effects or applauded for their uplifting potential. Music can be transcendent, touching our deepest emotions and changing our awareness. Popular culture—from the advertiser using ubiquitous jingles to the filmmaker spending hundreds of thousands of dollars on a movie soundtrack—understands the power of music. In its form, text, melody and harmony, music communicates in sensual, elemental ways. Music makes an amazing difference in how we enjoy the Mass.

It is wrong to talk about music at Mass as simply a nice addition, decorative effect or inconsequential element. Catholic liturgical documents insist that music is not an enhancement to prayer; it *is* prayer. I have celebrated liturgies at conferences and other special gatherings in which every person sings from the heart. The experience of singing as one voice, of blending together in one shout of praise, is overwhelming. When we unite our voices in sung prayer, we express our unity as the Body of Christ and experience and strengthen the oneness such unity implies.

The most beautiful and inspiring music requires a range of voices, timbres, instruments and textures. When we create harmony with diverse voices and instruments, we express the diversity of our gifts in service to God and one another. As we transcend gender, ethnicity, sexual orientation and age to create soul-filled music, we also strengthen our belief that such harmony is possible outside of the church building. We create the reality about which we preach. We live and appreciate the experience of unity in diversity, and we hunger for more.

What Was That Song About?

The texts of our liturgical songs are highly significant. Try reading the lyrics out loud and notice the prayers they contain. You may notice a difference in focus similar to the different body postures for prayer. Some hymns are penitential or meditative, some are joyous or full of gratitude, and some focus on a particular ritual action. Regardless, when we sing the texts of our prayers, the words affect us in conscious and unconscious ways. When we sing, the words both express and shape our theology.

If, for instance, our songs speak only of our personal relationship with God, if they are filled with "me" instead of "we," they run contrary to the purpose of the liturgy itself. Such songs may be wonderful evangelical songs, or they may deepen our personal spirituality, but they are not often appropriate in liturgical settings. Likewise, if the words of our songs constantly direct us inward to personal conversion but rarely direct us outward to our sisters and brothers who are oppressed and in need, they are not proper liturgical songs.

In liturgy, we become ever more who we are as the Body of Christ, but not for our own private benefit. As the hands, feet, face and arms of Christ, we are to change the world as Christ commands. Music can help us do that, and indeed liturgical music *must* help us do that.

The Assembly Performs

On occasion, a meditative solo can be appropriate during liturgy. For instance, I remember being deeply moved by the solo singing of the *Ave Maria* on the Feast of the Annunciation. Overall, though, the Mass is not a place for individual performance or passive appreciation of the musical gifts that other people possess—however considerable those gifts might be. Liturgical prayer is communal; therefore the music, integral to our prayer, is also communal. The cantor and other members of the choir are not called to perform but to lead the assembly into sung prayer. They are to set in motion, promote and support the liturgical action and the participation of the entire gathered assembly.

Of course, no one is encouraged to participate by a cantor who can't keep the beat or stay on key. Music ministers need to be competent in order to lead the prayer well. Still, the musical focus should be on the people as a whole—on the one "choir" that is formed by the cantors, musicians, presider, ministers and assembly together. This is a choir enclosed only by the walls of the church, walls that we hope will one day be transcended so the entire world may join in the singing.

Congregational singing is one of the criteria for good liturgy. Sung participation by all is not so much a duty as a gift and a joy that adds to the celebration. Imagine a birthday party where everyone is invited to *recite* the Happy Birthday song, or where each person has to sing it individually, or where everyone claims to have a bad voice and refuses to sing. The party would be ruined. It wouldn't work because singing—together and enthusiastically—is required for true celebration.

Likewise, God doesn't require or even expect musical perfection. We are called along with each member of the assembly to join with the musicians and to participate fully, singing whole-heartedly regardless of musical ability or training. God asks us to suspend judgment, both of ourselves and of one another, and raise our voices together in praise, in sorrow, in plea and in thanksgiving. When Christians gather to celebrate liturgy, it is the community that performs.

Questions for Discussion and Reflection

1. The next time you sit in private prayer at home, try changing your body posture. If you would normally kneel, try standing. If you would normally hold your hands together at your chest, try the *orans* position. How does it feel? How does your body posture affect your prayer?

2. When you celebrate Mass, pay close attention to the postures adopted by the assembly, the presider, the lector and other ministers during various parts of the ritual. What do those postures signify? If you were writing the liturgical rubrics, are there any postures you would change at certain parts of the Mass? What are they, and why would you change them?

3. Would you classify your parish as a singing assembly? How do you feel about the quality of your own singing voice? What do you think would help people be more comfortable singing wholeheartedly together?

4. Have you ever noticed someone in the assembly who has a very good voice and seems to want everyone else to hear it? What effect does his or her "over-singing" have on other people?

5. Read the lyrics of your favorite hymns and songs. What kind of prayers are they? Do the words express what you and your community want to say to God?

Chapter Seven

Community Counts

As the Body of Christ, we have both a corporate identity and a corporate mission. We are part of a universal Church, one that encircles the globe and is meant as a light for all nations. As the head of this Church, Jesus commands us to go into the world to help bring about the reign of God.

It is impossible to carry on this mission alone, however, especially in our complex and troubled world. The news reports are filled with difficulties and distraction, with war and violence, with scandal and broken trust. How are we to live justly in the midst of so much injustice? How can we preach forgiveness and reconciliation in a world where vengeance and war, power and might are promoted as the way to solve problems? How can we attempt to live simply in the midst of materialism and conspicuous consumption? How can we learn to welcome strangers when we are constantly told to fear them?

To change our lives, especially to follow the biblical commands to repent, convert and reconcile, we depend on the grace of God and need the help and support of others. The dynamic is similar to that of Alcoholics Anonymous, Weight Watchers and other programs. They work because they are group efforts in which people support and encourage one another. When we gather at Mass, we join with others who are also trying to live the gospel as faithful disciples. As we invite God to continue working in us, we gain assurance that we are not alone, that we are all members of the one Body and share in the one Spirit.

Over and over again in the Scriptures, we hear that individualism—looking out for our own interests, no matter what—will never ultimately work for us or for our world. We need to overcome our differences and disagreements and gather as the Body of Christ, focused on the God who unites us instead of the human things that separate us. We need to know that we are part of a larger story and a bigger picture and that—in spite of the doom and gloom around us—God will have the last word, and it will be the word of life.

So we come together at Mass as a sinful people before our God, broken and needy, hungry and thirsty for the word and the bread that give us life. We each participate with our whole heart—moving and praying and singing, responding as Christ would have us do. And wonder of wonders, we find ourselves slowly but surely transformed.

Where Would I Be without You?

Sharing a common experience, especially if it is deeply felt, is a powerful bond. The more central the experience, the tighter the bond will be. People who survive a life-threatening encounter, for instance, usually report that it brings them instantly closer. I facilitate discussion in a support group for those who are widowed. Members range widely in age, economic status and interests, yet the common experience of death forges friendships and attachments I never would have expected. People who become emotionally and intellectually engaged with one another become part of something bigger than themselves. They "feed" each other and feel connected.

As we gather for the liturgy, we come to express who we are—the visible Body of Christ in the world—and to be strengthened in that identity. What we experience together at Mass has the power to bond us as community and to transform our lives. We do not come to pray in isolation, closed off from those around us. We do not come to Mass just to pray our private prayers or have our personal time with God. We come to live out what we signify, to practice what we are called to be in the world. If, for instance, we declare ourselves to be a community but sit only near our friends, refuse to shake hands with others or do so reluctantly, and do not forgive one another from our hearts, our profession of faith is meaningless and we will not be transformed as we leave the church.

Come Sit at My Table

When we sing the national anthem together, unity is implied. It doesn't mean we don't have political issues, tensions and strident disagreements with one another. However, it does mean we have the ability to transcend our differences. Likewise, the Mass is one of the major elements of Catholic unity. It does not mean that we are all one in our thinking, opinions and beliefs. In fact, we Catholics probably have more theological diversity in our ranks than any other religious denomination. Yet the Mass not only allows but also encourages us to realize what we have in common as members of the Body of Christ. Our worth, our calling and our very identity come from our communal relationship to Christ, symbolized by our sharing of the one bread and the one cup. From this comes the strength we need to deal with our diversity in respectful and life-giving ways.

At Mass, then, we are not intended to get together with only people we like, or only those who are like us. We come with our brothers and sisters, each arriving from a different direction, each bringing concerns and life stories of their own, each a member of a different economic and ethnic structure, each of a different age and outlook. At liturgy, we welcome people who might not normally be our friends. Our baptism forms the bond between us, so the divisions created by society are irrelevant. The rich sit by the poor, those living with disabilities sit by the able-bodied, the single sit by the married, the jobless sit by the employed, the teens sit by the elderly. All of us join together to raise our voices in praise to the God who created us, saves us and sustains us.

An Arm or a Leg?

Jesus died over two thousand years ago. He now has no physical hands, eyes, face or body on this earth—except for yours and mine. If Christ wants to give someone a hug, it can't happen without our willingness to extend love to another. If Christ knows there is someone who needs a smile, one of us has to offer that smile. We are, literally and figuratively, the visible

Body of Christ on earth.

As members of Christ's Body, however, we do not all fill the same function. We each have been given unique talents and abilities. You contribute things to the rest of the Body that only you can give. No one else sees the world or experiences God in quite the same way as you do. No one else has your inimitable combination of gifts. No one else can bring to the assembly what you bring.

In a particular liturgy some individuals fill more visible roles, yet none of us is more important than any other. How can a lector proclaim Scripture if there is no one to hear? The presider cannot "preside" over empty pews. As Saint Paul wrote to the Corinthians, "If the whole body were an eye, where would the hearing be? If the whole body were hearing, where would be the sense of smell? But as it is, God arranged the members of the body, each one of them, as he chose" (1 Corinthians 12:17-18). All of us are essential to the celebration of the Mass.

Likewise, in our lives outside the liturgy, we fulfill a range of functions and serve God and one another in various ways. No one person can do it all. You are called to do what you have the gifts and talents to do, leaving other tasks to those with other gifts and vocations. In our wondrous diversity, we form the many parts of Christ's Body and fulfill all the roles that are necessary for that Body to function.

Where Did You Go?

I have nine brothers and sisters and twenty-one nieces and nephews, and we love to get together whenever we can. In fact, being a family necessitates getting together. Gathering and celebrating is part of what forms our identity as a family, builds our relationships with one another, and molds us into a cohesive group. Even when a few of us are not able to join the gathering, there are still plenty of people there. We still celebrate and have a good time. But for each of us, it isn't the same without those who are absent. There is an empty space, a hole that only those people can fill. What we do as a family takes all of us. It is the same with the Mass.

I have heard many people insist that they can skip Mass and not miss out on anything. That is a misunderstanding. If you don't gather for Mass on a particular Sabbath, you miss out on being with the rest of the Body of Christ that week, and your absence lessens the experience for everyone who is there. The words *company* and *companion* mean "those with whom you break bread." If you are not there, others cannot break bread with you and their experience is in some way diminished. It can be harder to feel this dynamic in very large parishes, where members of the assembly sometimes feel like anonymous elements of the crowd. Yet even in that case, each person brings his or her uniqueness to the celebration. If you are not there, in other words, it literally won't be the same without you!

Sometimes Our Instruments Are Out of Tune

People sometimes disengage from Mass because liturgy isn't done well in their parish. What we Catholics have to remember is that our priests and other ministers are first and foremost human beings. The priest may not pray the prayers as well or with as much sincerity as we'd like. His homily may not be as inspiring or thought-provoking as we'd hoped. The cantor may be slightly off key or too quiet for us to hear clearly. The lector may not proclaim the Scriptures effectively. We can be tempted to sit in the pew and criticize, concentrating on how these imperfect ministers keep us from Christ instead of leading us closer to him.

When we do that, of course, God's action in us is blocked. The Spirit of God is all around us, longing to pour grace and peace into our hearts. God may act strongly in our lives or even knock us off our proverbial horse, but we still have free will to accept or reject what is offered. It is like the electricity that is constantly flowing through wires in the walls all around us. We aren't usually aware that the electricity is there, nor are we able to realize the benefits it provides, unless we *plug in*. When God's Spirit does not connect with us through the presider or one of the other ministers, instead of bemoaning the ineffective outlet we simply need to find another way to plug in.

Perhaps you are called to help the ministers be better instruments of God. If you yourself were the presider or a minister with a visible role, I doubt you would be perfect. I imagine, though, you would appreciate the feedback of people in the assembly, telling you what you do well and where you still need work. Take the energy you would spend complaining and use it instead to find ways to help the "electricity" flow freely.

Prepare to Celebrate

Because the liturgy is a repeated ritual, it is easy to lapse into over-familiarity or even indifference. After all, we all know what is going to happen, right down to the final "Amen." But as we have seen in this book, the Mass is different every single time, and we need to take it as seriously as we take other important events in our lives.

For instance, I know a couple with season tickets to the symphony. They are avid fans of classical music and thoroughly enjoy the performances they attend. However, they never attend a concert without preparing ahead of time. During the week prior to a concert, the couple looks up the musical selections that will be played. Using the Internet and the local library, they research the composers and the compositions so they can understand the genre, structure and historicity of the music. If they own the appropriate recordings, they listen to them at least once or twice. They discuss what they notice in the music, what they feel during different movements, and how the pieces connect with one another.

By the time this couple attends the symphony, they are well-prepared and flushed with excitement over what they are about to hear. They immerse themselves in the music, carried by the rhythms and caught up into an experience that transcends their daily lives. At the end of the evening, they feel they have touched the divine in the gift of humanly created music. Their souls are refreshed, and they have already begun to anticipate the next concert.

Few people attend so closely to their experience of the

Mass. All too often, we rush to get there on time, perhaps arriving a few minutes late. Breathlessly, we sit down in the pew and try to pray or listen to the readings while our minds are still recalling the hectic trip or noticing whether the children are properly behaved or running down the list of activities to be done following the Mass. We allow the familiar routine to brush by us with little notice. Sometimes we perk up at the homily (if it is engaging) and then return to automatic pilot until the Lord's Prayer and Communion. By that time, we know Mass is almost over and may struggle to maintain our attention. When liturgy ends and we are sent forth, we often leave with a sigh of relief. Most of the time we remember little from the service or the readings. We are the same when we leave Mass as we were when we entered. No true transformation has taken place in our minds or hearts, and therefore not much changes in our attitudes or actions.

In other words, some of us still come to Mass on Sunday in a passive frame of mind, expecting to have something done *to* or *for* us. But just as poor preparation on the part of our ministers can damage or destroy the celebration, poor preparation and participation by those of us in the assembly can render the Mass boring and inert. So take the time to make sure you are as prepared for the Mass as you would like the presider, homilist, lectors, musicians and other ministers to be.

What would happen if you spent just a few minutes of time during the week preparing yourself to celebrate Sunday Mass? Like the couple going to the symphony, start by looking at the readings a week ahead of time. Read them out loud, with your family or on your own, and notice the characters, the story line, and especially any surprising twists or challenges. Decide whether and how the three readings relate to one another, and reflect on possible lessons you would preach about if you were to give the homily. Put yourself in the place of one of the characters and describe the experience from your own point of view. If time allows, take advantage of a user-friendly Scripture guide to do a little research on the authors of the readings and the audience to whom they were writing.

As you read and think about the Scriptures, place them in

the context of the liturgical season. Is it a Sunday in the Easter season; Lent or Ordinary Time; a special feast? How do the readings connect with the readings from the previous week?

When Sunday arrives, plan your time so that you arrive for Mass at least five or ten minutes early. (If your spouse or kids object to this, go to church ahead of them and save a pew for the family.) After greeting or visiting with people as you enter the church, make sure you have a music book or worship aid. If the hymns are posted, read the lyrics and see how they relate to the readings and the feast or season being celebrated. Enjoy the environment—the colors and the mood of the worship space— and let yourself settle into it. Say a brief prayer that you will be open to God's working in your life through this liturgy and that your participation will enrich both your own spirituality and the liturgical experience of the community.

When Mass begins, be ready and alert, excited about what is to come. Appreciate the procession, the vestments and the candles. Experience the symbols and gestures of prayer with deep-felt meaning. Listen carefully to the readings, taking the message to heart. Be attentive to the homily and interested in whether the preacher chooses the same images you might have chosen. Let the gift of yourself be placed on the altar with the gifts of bread and wine. Feel the rhythm of the Eucharistic Prayer and sing the responses heartily. Join in the recitation of the Lord's Prayer with the community and come to the table to be fed and strengthened for the journey. Finally, accept your mission to live out—on your job, with your family, and in your community and civic activities—what you have just experienced within the community of believers.

Imagine how different our celebration would be if we prepared and participated like this. Even the stodgiest presider or the weakest Scripture proclamation can be overcome by prepared and open hearts that allow God to work. If we want to "get something out of the Mass" perhaps we should come prepared to fully celebrate it.

Sacramental Action

Sacraments are not things; they are actions. They are actions of Christ, actions of the Church, and actions of those who celebrate them. Although there are different levels of responsibility within a particular celebration, each of us present is in a very real way a minister of the sacrament. It is our duty and our right to celebrate fully, consciously and actively, to cooperate with God in making the sacrament come alive.

Celebrating people act differently from bored people. Celebrating people come to Mass prepared to pray, to hear God's word, to worship with the community, to be fed, and to be sent forth. Good or bad, imperfect or outstanding, the priest, the ministers and the assembly all worship together as celebrating people. And when the community celebrates well, we dispel boredom and disappointment and find ourselves truly becoming the Body of Christ.

Questions for Reflection and Discussion

1. Most people have events in their work or home lives that require substantial preparation. For what events in your life do you seriously prepare? What does your commitment say about the importance of those events?

2. When have you been seated at a table with someone very different from yourself? What did it feel like, and how did you handle the situation?

3. If you were to serve in one of the visible liturgical roles—as an usher, lector, cantor, choir member, extraordinary Eucharistic minister—which would you choose? How would you carry out your responsibilities in ways that help the community celebrate?

4. How much do you feel a part of your parish assembly? Do you believe someone would notice if you were not there? Do you notice when attendance is down or when people you usually see at Mass are absent? What can you do to be more aware of those with whom you celebrate?

5. Write an analysis of your parish celebration of the Mass. Share your thoughts with the pastor or presiders. Be sure to start with what is already being done well and only then offer some constructive ways things might be improved. Offer to help!

Chapter Eight

Get Outta Here

When Jesus was transfigured on the mountaintop, Peter didn't want the moment to end. He offered to build three tents—one for Jesus, one for Moses, and one for Elijah—so they could all stay there and allow the wonderful experience to continue. Jesus, however, had other ideas. As compelling as the experience on the mountain was, as much as it fed the spirits and inspired the faith of the disciples, the real mission was not in that place. They had to come down from the mountain and use the vision and wisdom they had gained to better serve God's people in the world.

So it is with the Mass. We gather as the Body of Christ, hear the stories that give us our roots and our future, offer thanks and praise to our God, and share the meal that makes us whole. It would be so comfortable to just stay put, safe within the walls and secure with people who share our beliefs and values. As Jesus reminds us, it is easy to love those who love us. But the church is not where we are called to remain. Rather, we are sent out into the world: "Go in peace to love and serve the Lord." In the Dismissal Rite, we are blessed and commissioned to take what we have received from the liturgy and go forth—changed, transformed, and ready to serve wherever God may lead us.

The word *Mass* is a derivation of the Latin word *missa*, which, in turn, comes from the word *mittere*, meaning "to send." It is the same root from which we get the words *mission*, *commission* and *dismiss*. In early forms of the liturgy, the Mass was ended with the Latin phrase *Ite, missa est. Ite* is a command that means "go" or "you, go." So the word-for-word translation of the phrase *Ite, missa est* is: "Go, it is sent." A logical translation is the command: "Go, you are sent on a mission." *The Mass* is thus a shorthand way of saying that the purpose of our gathering is to go out and continue the mission of Christ. When we are told, "Go in peace to love and serve the Lord," we hear echoes of Jesus telling his disciples to be his witnesses to the ends of the earth, to proclaim the Good News to all peoples, and to love one another as he has loved us. By using "the Mass," a word that comes directly from the Dismissal Rite, as the name of our Eucharistic Liturgy, we Catholics indicate just how seriously we take this commissioning. The end of the Mass is only the beginning of what we come together to do.

The Meaning Is in the Living

No sacrament exists as an end in itself. Although we leave the assembly and the church building, we carry something with us. We are transformed and nourished in the sacraments so that we might become sacraments to the world. It is not like going out from a play, where the hard work of practicing and performing are already finished. In the celebrations of the sacraments, we bring all that has come before, mingle it with a special liminal moment of the now, and anticipate a future toward which the moment is propelling us.

For example, the sacrament of matrimony is celebrated at a wedding. The couple brings the history of their courtship to the moment—their meeting, the budding of romance, the engagement, the planning, and all the dreams of their hearts. In a compelling and meaningful ritual, everything they are and everything they hope to be is expressed and intensified as the community joins together to witness the public commitment of their love and to provide them with support, wisdom and strength.

It is after the ceremony, though, that the hard work of being married really begins. What happens in the time after the wedding gives deeper meaning to the rings the couple exchanged and to the love they publicly expressed. They have to become what they professed during the wedding, learning to live fully as one and become what they promise to each other.

Likewise, celebrating Eucharist is only the beginning. We have to become what we rehearse, learning to fully live it out forever more. The difference between a wedding and Mass is that the Eucharist is a repeatable sacrament. We have the privilege of celebrating it every week, reminding us of what we are to do, opening us to God's action in our lives, and strengthening us for the task. Each Sunday we renew our initiation into the Catholic Christian community and intensify our commitment to live as members of that Body. We bring all that we are to the liturgy, where we express and celebrate it, and then we carry our new awareness into the next week.

What we do during the week gives deeper meaning to the ritual actions we have celebrated at Mass, and what we celebrate at Mass gives deeper meaning to what we do during the week. As we carry our own brokenness and minister to others who are hurting, we find more profound meaning and strength in receiving the broken bread in the Eucharist. As we pour out our lives in love for the homeless and the alienated, for our families and friends, for those considered "the least of these," we find meaning and strength in the blood poured out for us. It is in the interplay between the Mass and our everyday lives that the full impact of the liturgy is fulfilled.

At Least That's Over

In the procession out of the worship space, I recently heard one man declare to his wife, "There. I've put in my time." Having just experienced a meaningful and Spirit-filled celebration of the liturgy, I felt deep sadness at the man's words. He missed it. For him, Mass was a hoop to jump through in order to earn God's favor. He had obeyed the law, followed the rules, and made sure his body was present—even if his heart wasn't. God owed him now, and he would surely get his reward. By "putting in his time," he had earned his place in heaven.

Yet we know that salvation is not earned, nor can it ever be. Salvation is free, a gift from God. God lavishes grace and salvation upon us, not because we are worthy or have earned it by our good deeds but simply because God loves us. We come to liturgy to celebrate that gift, to be formed into Christ who gave his own life to reveal how much God loves us and to show us the path of discipleship.

The Mass is not so much about what *we do* as about what

God does in us. Liturgy is always leading us to transformation, especially to the difficult and life-altering transformation we cannot accomplish on our own. Yet this transformation is not something alien from us, something we have to do because God demands it. It is written in our hearts from the beginning, reflected in our deepest desires and longings. The transformation God seeks is one that allows us to become the best and most fulfilled human beings we can be. The transformation God seeks is one that brings us the peace, joy, love and hope for which we yearn. The transformation God seeks is one in which the divine will is done on earth as it is in heaven.

The Mass, then, is not about obeying rules but about responding in joy to the One who creates, calls and saves us in the first place. When we leave Mass, we go forth not as mindless robots that have to do the right things to please the Master. We go forth as beloved children who have become the very flesh and blood of Christ.

We *need* the Mass to help us do that. We *need* the Mass as a model of how we are to live the rest of our lives. We do not *attend* Mass out of obligation. We *celebrate* Mass to become who we are created to be.

A Dangerous Prayer

On more than one occasion when I shared prayer requests with my parents they told me, "Be careful what you ask for; you might get it!" Most of the time, they responded this way because I was not wise or mature enough to foresee the implications of my requests. While the request seemed reasonable from my perspective, they knew that I might not welcome the consequences if it were actually granted.

Do you realize what we ask for when we celebrate Mass? The liturgy, and especially the Eucharistic Prayer, is a most marvelous and dangerous prayer. We ask God to change us. We ask that we may follow in Christ's footsteps—and that means to the cross. We ask that we ourselves may become the body and blood of Christ poured out for the world. We ask that we may be truly joined as one, loving one another as Christ loves us. We ask that all divisions and barriers be broken down and that we live God's kingdom on earth.

In other words, the prayer in which we ask God to ensure that no child goes to bed hungry tonight is empty if we are not willing to do something ourselves to make that happen. Our prayer is empty if we ask for peace and tolerance in the world yet hold on to grudges, prejudices and retaliation. "Thy kingdom come" is an empty prayer if we are not willing to sacrifice ourselves to bring that kingdom into being.

We cannot pray in intimacy with our God nor take Christ's flesh and blood into ourselves without also being in intimate contact with those God loves. We are all creatures of the one Creator. We come from God and will return to God. Because we have the same source, the same precious blood flowing through our veins, we are connected not only to God but also to each other through God. As we are sent forth from the liturgy, we are called to respond to the concerns of the God who gives us life. Our prayer stirs us up, changes our hearts, and opens our eyes to the face of evil, violence, oppression, war and all that threatens the dignity of our brothers and sisters around the world. We are called to nothing less than to transform the human condition and make the world a place fit for all to inhabit.

The Door Never Closes

And so we go forth "to love and serve the Lord." Truly the power of the liturgy does not end at the church door. We are always the Body of Christ, always in communion with one another, always the Church. In each one of us, God is calling and blessing and sanctifying the world.

There is no division between liturgy and life. Our lives flow into and out of the liturgy, the source of our strength. *To* the liturgy we bring our stresses and successes, our worries and joys, our ups and downs. *In* the liturgy we are consecrated, fed and strengthened. *From* the liturgy we are sent forth to be Christ to the world. It is like oxygen-depleted blood flowing through the heart and lungs so it can be pumped back out to bring nourishment and life to the entire body.

Those of us gathered for the Eucharist are the same people Christ has chosen to carry on his mission. We who hear the word of God are sent forth to live the word throughout the week. We who praise God are sent forth to bring God to others. We who have given thanks at the table of the liturgy are sent forth to give thanks over all of our tables and meals. We who receive the body and blood of Christ are sent forth to be Christ to one another. We who have practiced discipleship in the liturgy are sent forth to bring the liturgy into the world.

What we have received cannot be contained within the walls of the church building. Having proclaimed and celebrated the wondrous acts of God and opened ourselves to God's workings in our hearts, we are sent forth to take on the responsibility entrusted to us by Christ: to proclaim the Good News to the world, feeding the hungry, clothing the poor, comforting the brokenhearted, visiting the sick and imprisoned, and bringing about the reign of God.

The Conversion Continues

We live in a very human Church made up of imperfect, finite creatures. Although God's Spirit is always with us, always guiding us, always tugging us, we can be hard of hearing and slow of heart.

I am aware that through most of this book, I have spoken of liturgy as it is ideally intended to be. I am also painfully aware of how often we fall short of this ideal. There are far too many Masses being *tolerated* rather than *celebrated*. Far too many teenagers and young people experience Mass as a boring, dead ritual. Far too many priests and liturgical ministers seem to be going through the motions without any spirit.

Most of this lifelessness can be traced to a lack of understanding, both of the Mass itself and of each person's role in it. Lack of understanding leads to poor ministerial leadership, including presiders who don't preside or preach well, songs that are not intended for the assembly to sing, and lectors who read Scripture as if it were a page from the *Wall Street Journal*. It also leads to poor assembly participation—an attitude of passivity, responses that are mumbled into the air, and the reciting of the Creed or the Lord's Prayer with all the gusto of a jury summons.

I do believe, however, that the liturgy can be a powerful, transformative experience when it is done well. The task before us is to help people understand why and how this is possible. It is our task to bring renewed light and life to the central ritual of our faith.

So, just as the end of the Mass is only the beginning of the story, so too the end of this book is only the beginning. My hope is that because of the insights and information contained herein, your celebration of the Mass will change. You will enter with increased awareness and understanding into the celebration, and by your example you will help others do so as well. You will accept the challenge to consciously and actively participate in the Mass, taking in the word and the meal in order to live out what you receive in the rest of your life. It is only in doing so, and in helping others do the same, that the power of this marvelous ritual will be fulfilled.

Questions for Reflection and Discussion

1. Have you ever attended a motivational class or seminar and left excited about the change it would make in your life? How long did the effect actually last? Have you ever returned for a "refresher"? Why or why not?

2. Listen to the words of the Eucharistic Prayers. What parts sound "dangerous" or difficult to live out?

3. Name at least two concrete actions you can take that will help you carry the liturgy with you into your daily life.

4. If God's kingdom truly came on earth, how would your life and your lifestyle be different? What things are blocking you from helping to bring the reign of God into being?

5. Imagine explaining the Mass to someone who has never heard of it before. List the five most important points you would try to cover.

Acknowledgments

A book is never a solo venture. There are many people without whom I could not have created this little tome and to whom I am most grateful.

Rory Cooney constantly blessed me with invaluable advice and insight from his wealth of knowledge as a liturgist and a musician. Stephen Schmidt read the text as an objective non-Catholic theology professor, wisely pointing out where clarification and revisions were needed.

Encouragement and support came from my friends and colleagues, especially Maureen Donohue, Theresa Donohoo, Gary Daigle and Terry Wessels. My parents, Bud and Jane Ross, read every word, offering perspective from the pew as well as the unconditional love that only parents can give.

Finally, my husband Ken, the light of my life and my greatest cheerleader, stood by me, put up with me, and loved me through it all.

To each of these, I offer my wholehearted gratitude.